ROUTLEDGE LIBRARY EDITIONS:
NUCLEAR SECURITY

Volume 26

ARMS CONTROL

ARMS CONTROL
Management or Reform?

LAWRENCE FREEDMAN

LONDON AND NEW YORK

First published in 1986 by Routledge & Kegan Paul Ltd

This edition first published in 2021
by Routledge
2 Park Square, Milton Park, Abingdon, Oxon OX14 4RN

and by Routledge
52 Vanderbilt Avenue, New York, NY 10017

Routledge is an imprint of the Taylor & Francis Group, an informa business

© 1986 Royal Institute of International Affairs

All rights reserved. No part of this book may be reprinted or reproduced or utilised in any form or by any electronic, mechanical, or other means, now known or hereafter invented, including photocopying and recording, or in any information storage or retrieval system, without permission in writing from the publishers.

Trademark notice: Product or corporate names may be trademarks or registered trademarks, and are used only for identification and explanation without intent to infringe.

British Library Cataloguing in Publication Data
A catalogue record for this book is available from the British Library

ISBN: 978-0-367-50682-7 (Set)
ISBN: 978-1-00-309763-1 (Set) (ebk)
ISBN: 978-0-367-55075-2 (Volume 26) (hbk)
ISBN: 978-1-00-309190-5 (Volume 26) (ebk)

Publisher's Note
The publisher has gone to great lengths to ensure the quality of this reprint but points out that some imperfections in the original copies may be apparent.

Disclaimer
The publisher has made every effort to trace copyright holders and would welcome correspondence from those they have been unable to trace.

CHATHAM HOUSE PAPERS · 31

ARMS CONTROL
MANAGEMENT OR REFORM?

Lawrence Freedman

The Royal Institute of International Affairs

Routledge & Kegan Paul
London, New York and Henley

The Royal Institute of International Affairs is an unofficial body which promotes the scientific study of international questions and does not express opinions of its own. The opinions expressed in this paper are the responsibility of the author.

First published 1986
by Routledge & Kegan Paul Ltd
11 New Fetter Lane, London EC4P 4EE
29 West 35th Street, New York, NY 10001, USA

Set by Hope Services, Abingdon and
printed in Great Britain by
Billing and Son Ltd, Worcester

© Royal Institute of International Affairs 1986

No part of this book may be reproduced in any form without permission from the publisher, except for the quotation of brief passages in criticism.

Library of Congress Cataloging-in-Publication Data

Freedman, Lawrence.
Arms control.

(Chatham House papers : 31)
   'The Royal Institute of International Affairs.'
   1. Nuclear arms control—United States. 2. Nuclear arms control—Soviet Union. 3. Negotiation.
4. Security, International. 5. Europe—Defenses.
I. Royal Institute of International Affairs.
II. Title. III. Series.
JX1974.7.F725   1986   327.1'74   86-15587
ISBN 0-7102-0893-6

CONTENTS

Abbreviations / vi
Preface / vii
1 Introduction / 1
2 The objectives of arms control / 5
3 The political context / 12
4 Parity and sufficiency / 19
5 Strategic arms control / 25
6 Intermediate nuclear forces / 35
7 Mutual and balanced force reductions / 47
8 Confidence-building measures / 53
9 Conclusion / 69

Appendices
1 Negotiating history of SALT / 75
2 Negotiating history of START / 77
3 Negotiating history of INF / 80
4 The data question in INF / 86
5 Negotiating history of MBFR / 89
6 The data question in MBFR / 95
7 Negotiating history of the Conference on Confidence and Security Building Measures and Disarmament / 98

ABBREVIATIONS

ABM	Anti-Ballistic Missile
ALCM	Air-Launched Cruise Missile
CBMs	Confidence-Building Measures
CDE	Conference on Disarmament in Europe
CSCE	Conference on Security and Cooperation in Europe
GLCM	Ground-Launched Cruise Missile
ICBM	Intercontinental Ballistic Missile
INF	Intermediate Nuclear Forces
IRBM	Intermediate-Range Ballistic Missile
MAD	Mutual Assured Destruction
MBFR	Mutual and Balanced Force Reductions
MIRV	Multiple Independently Targetable Re-entry Vehicle
MX	Missile Experimental
NATO	North Atlantic Treaty Organization
NNA	Neutral and Non-Aligned (countries)
SALT	Strategic Arms Limitation Talks
SDI	Strategic Defence Initiative
SLBM	Submarine-Launched Ballistic Missile
SSBN	Ballistic-Missile-Carrying Nuclear Submarine
START	Strategic Arms Reduction Talks

PREFACE

This paper began as a revision of a Chatham House Paper published in 1981 on *Arms Control in Europe*. The revision turned out to be more substantial than I originally anticipated, so that this, in most respects, is a new paper. The experience of the intervening years suggested many areas in which the argument needed sharpening. It has also been an eventful, if not especially productive, few years for arms control, which encouraged me to concentrate on the most prominent of recent developments and trends.

One of the problems with arms control is that the detail can soon become overwhelming. Unfortunately much of the detail is also important. I have dealt with this problem by relegating background descriptions of the negotiations to a series of appendices, which I hope will be found useful for reference purposes.

I am very grateful to a study group, organized by the Royal Institute of International Affairs, whose discussion of an earlier draft led to considerable modification and amendment, and also to those students who have taken my arms control course at King's College and have helped me more than I have let them realize! It has been a special pleasure to work again with two friends and former colleagues from Chatham House — Joan Pearce and Pauline Wickham — whose combined editorial talents are quite formidable. Thanks are also due to Nigel Pearce for his work on the manuscript.

June 1986 L.F.

1
INTRODUCTION

In the aftermath of the November 1985 summit between President Ronald Reagan and General-Secretary Mikhail Gorbachev, arms control was widely seen to be back on track. The lack of progress in building on the 'spirit' of that summit during the first few months of 1986 dampened enthusiasm, but it is still generally felt that the major powers are embarked on a serious negotiating exercise that could well produce results over the next few years.

Much of this paper is taken up with examining this exercise and the issues being addressed. It draws attention to the many problems still to be overcome if agreements are to be reached, as well as to the areas of possible compromise that have already become apparent. It also offers a critical analysis of the arms control process. The line of argument developed here is not that of the hawk who complains that arms control has served only as an instrument of Soviet policy by lulling us into a false sense of security and so providing an excuse for avoiding military preparedness. Nor is it that of the dove who points contemptuously to collections of permissive ceilings and marginal constraints which barely inconvenience military planners and are merely superpower confidence tricks reflecting the lack of political will to stop the arms race.

Rather, the analysis highlights the confusion surrounding the objectives of arms control, and the effects of this confusion on the practice. The objectives are often taken for granted, on the assumption that it is the degree of mistrust separating the two sides that determines the extent to which the objectives can be met.

Introduction

Closer examination, however, soon reveals that arms control is pursued for many different reasons, which are by no means always in concert. There is also a tension between two alternative approaches, which do not so much separate East from West as the reformers from the managers — hence the title of this essay.

To the reformers, arms control is worthwhile only if it produces major changes in the international system. The Reagan administration, for example, has argued that negotiations to achieve strategic arms *limitations*, and so merely consolidate the status quo, are pointless. The minimum aim must be to *reduce*. Together with Mr Gorbachev, President Reagan has agreed that the objective must be to eliminate nuclear weapons from the earth, and Mr Gorbachev has even provided a timetable for achieving this by the end of the century. Such a goal would be music to the ears of the many non-governmental groups that campaign vigorously for disarmament, had they not heard political leaders express similar sentiments so often in the past. But these groups are in no doubt that this is the direction in which the politicians must be pushed. They hope that a virtuous cycle can be created: the arms race is seen as the source of superpower antagonism; put the arms race into reverse and a reduction in antagonism should follow.

By contrast, the managers argue that the East-West antagonism derives from genuine conflicts of interests and ideology, and that it will therefore persist until these conflicts are resolved. It is much more than a creature of the arms race. Furthermore, talk of eliminating nuclear weapons from the earth is utopian. The secret is out. There could never be a situation in which there could be confidence that *all* potentially hostile powers both lacked nuclear weapons and could not develop them during the course of a conflict. Moreover, many of this persuasion would argue that even if such a situation were achieved, it would not necessarily be an improvement. The current position is one where war between the major powers has been effectively deterred through fear of the nuclear consequences. The effort to bring arsenals down to zero could be extremely destabilizing in itself, for as the levels get lower the significance of individual weapons becomes greater. In a world of nuclear plenty, a few extra weapons make little difference. In a world that was ostensibly nuclear-free, these same weapons could make *all* the difference. The managers therefore argue that the objective of arms control is not to change a basically satisfactory status quo but to ensure that the antagonism does not get out of hand, so that even the most intense crisis can be survived without disaster.

Unfortunately for both the reformers and the managers, the actual consequences of arms control are often different from those that either group might prefer. The arms control process itself — the internal bureaucratic round, the proposals and counter-proposals, the formal and informal negotiations, the summits — can be as significant in its effects as any of the agreements that might emerge, especially as agreements have been few and far between. The process may promote greater harmony all round, but it also often serves to sharpen tensions within governments and alliances, not to mention those between traditional adversaries. It provides opportunities for deflecting as well as promoting far-reaching reforms. More seriously, the interaction between arms control and the development of military capabilities and strategic doctrines can produce curious and perplexing results. When, as has been the case recently, strategic doctrine becomes controversial, the debate occasioned by the arms control process can expose internal contradictions and encourage shifts in military policy.

It is important that any approach to arms control takes all this into account. To mention ways in which the arms control process can be counterproductive is not to deny its many positive features. It provides a means of ensuring that the great powers talk to each other about their security concerns. In principle, it also provides an opportunity to reduce the level of armaments and military expenditure, to head off dangerous new weapons developments and to create the conditions for preventing future crises from turning into war.

At any rate, arms control is now too much a part of international life to be abandoned. In one form or another it will be with us for some time. It cannot in itself be an instrument of political or military reform; it will work best in support of other measures designed to ease East-West relations and improve the overall security position or reinforce general trends working in those directions. Inevitably it is easier and often more valuable for arms control to be used for the purposes of management than of reform. What must be guarded against is arms control serving as a drag on desirable changes or, worse still, channelling change into undesirable areas. The need, therefore, is to clarify objectives, not only

Introduction

for the sake of arms control but for security policy in general.

This is especially important for those West European governments that have encouraged the view that multilateral arms control can succeed where unilateral disarmament would only be counter-productive — both in slowing down the arms race and in relaxing East-West relations. In recent years, though, an anxiety for visible signs of progress has resulted in uncritical enthusiasm for any negotiating activity regardless of its content. This activity may have helped in terms of political management, but it has raised a promise of military reform that is unlikely to be fulfilled. The political value of negotiations will decline if they continue to fail to reach a conclusion; if they are to conclude with agreements, their *strategic* consequences must be addressed.

2
THE OBJECTIVES OF ARMS CONTROL

Our inquiry can begin with an examination of the strategic benefits that might be obtained through arms control. These can best be explored by looking at arms control theory, which developed in the late 1950s and early 1960s in response to the combination of a cold war and a nuclear arms race. The theory was based on a simple insight: despite their deep-rooted antagonism, East and West shared a critical interest in avoiding war, particularly nuclear war. Through tacit or explicit understandings, the two antagonists should work to avoid military confrontation: better to accept a stalemate than to prepare for a decisive — but probably catastrophic — showdown.

Because the underlying ideological, political and economic differences were not to be resolved, only kept in check, there was no obvious point at which the antagonism ended and the sense of shared interest began. This created the challenge for the theory. The point of transformation had to be defined accurately, and with confidence that the other side would not see the antagonism lasting a little longer and the shared interest coming later.

Agreements building upon the common interest, the argument ran, could emerge in one of two ways. One possibility was to rely on an understanding evolving naturally out of the logic of diplomacy at those moments of crisis when continued antagonism could lead to immediate disaster. However, it was risky to depend on wise statecraft in circumstances of high tension and danger; the necessary understanding might arrive too late and be too ambiguous and too tenuous. The other possibility was to negotiate agreements

The objectives of arms control

prior to a crisis at a time of normal international relations. This would leave far less to chance, but the difficulty remained that the negotiating conditions of 'normal' international affairs were still those of 'normal' antagonism, even if not of the heightened tension of a crisis. There would still be mutual suspicion.

The persistence of the antagonism would always be reflected in military capabilities. Force levels could be reduced, but they would never reach zero. So disarmament could not eliminate the risk of the antagonism spilling over into war. In practice, therefore, it was always necessary to be prepared to conduct a prudent crisis diplomacy. The most that prior agreements could offer was either a degree of 'crisis stability' or else partial disarmament, and that if war did break out it would be fought at a lower level than would otherwise have been the case. Arms controllers were managers, whose priority was crisis stability.

Crisis stability

According to the concept of crisis stability, the tempo of diplomacy and the search for political settlement need not be driven mercilessly by the tempo of military preparations and the fear of pre-emptive attack. A stable military relationship is one in which neither side can expect a lasting profit by actually initiating war. The principle is that no war must be allowed to start because of some military imperative before all diplomatic options have been exhausted. It must be possible to hold back on military action without fear of being caught by an early mobilization or a surprise attack.

This fear developed in the 1950s as a result of developments in nuclear weapons technology that were putting a premium on a first strike. 'Victory' in nuclear war could be achieved only by destroying the adversary's capacity for retaliation in a disarming, pre-emptive strike and/or by catching any forces, once launched, by means of effective active defences. The risk here was of a crisis getting out of control as each side fretted about its vulnerability to enemy pre-emption.

The hope was that the balance of terror, though uncomfortable, would remain stable if properly managed. The essential condition came to be known as 'mutual assured destruction' (MAD), which

The objectives of arms control

was never intended to describe the ultimate fate of the protagonists, only to emphasize an ever-present possibility. So long as both sides were aware that any destruction would be 'mutual' and 'assured', they would always hold their nuclear fire. Something less mutual and less assured might just tempt one side into a rash gamble.

In the end, avoiding war depends on political judgment at critical moments and cannot be guaranteed by any particular configuration of military forces. Nevertheless the prospect of mutual destruction does seem to have had a sobering effect. US and Soviet forces have yet to meet in battle or even mild skirmish, despite the turbulence and periodic crises of the post-1945 world. The sense of shared interest in war-avoidance has thankfully made a deep impression on national leaders.

The need for active negotiations depends on the extent to which the independent development of military forces displays an inherent bias towards instability. Talk about an 'arms race' assumes that one exists, and so generates demands for positive action to correct the bias and reverse the 'mad momentum'. However, analysis of the actual pattern of postwar military developments provides a more complex and, in some ways, more comforting picture. Certainly weapons have become individually more lethal, more ingenious and more destructive. Nevertheless, taken together, they have confirmed the military paralysis by ensuring that any initiation of hostilities could not result in easy victory or eliminate the risk of enormous cost and general catastrophe.

This position has been reinforced by stabilizing measures that required little by way of direct negotiation. Both sides have taken steps to avoid a loss of control over *national* forces in a crisis, and to offer too tempting a set of targets to the adversary. Command and control mechanisms have been improved so as to reduce the risks of accidental launches of nuclear weapons, and systems have been adopted that can 'ride out' a first strike and so reduce pressure to launch on warning or pre-empt. In the United States these measures have been well publicized in the hope that the Soviet Union would follow the example.

Because of the self-evident value of protecting at least one part of the deterrent from surprise attack, little encouragement was needed to develop ballistic-missile-carrying nuclear submarines (SSBNs). Because SSBNs are relatively invulnerable and, at least up to now, their missiles have been too inaccurate for first strikes against the adversary, their introduction established the sort of strategic relationship required by arms control theory. With a secure means of retaliation, there could be no military premium in launching a surprise attack.

Mutual assured destruction was further reinforced by the difficulties experienced in developing ballistic missile defences. In the 1960s both superpowers embarked on defensive programmes which, if successful, might have had a disturbing impact on the strategic balance by making destruction less assured. As it turned out, the major advances in radar, computing and interception during the 1960s were trumped by advances in offensive capabilities, particularly multiple independently targetable re-entry vehicles (MIRVs).

If we consider arms control in terms of crisis stability, as a description of a type of strategic relationship rather than as a set of negotiating efforts, then we already have arms control, in a healthy and robust form, and have enjoyed it for much of the past three decades. This raises questions about the purposes of the negotiating exercise. One does not rush forward to tune a TV set which is working perfectly by itself; to do so may just make a clear picture fuzzy. According to the classical theory, the purpose of arms control is solely to adjust the strategic relationship in order to restore equilibrium, or prevent its being lost. Once in equilibrium, the relationship should be left alone and energies should be devoted to other tasks.

Arms race stability

A secondary objective of arms control, which may require more by way of actual negotiating activity, is the pursuit of arms race stability. Arms race stability is more concerned with preventing peacetime rivalries from creating a crisis than with what to do should the crisis arise. The goal is to stop arms competition getting out of hand in the event of both sides overexerting themselves for fear that the other might be gaining an advantage.

The case for arms race stability begins with an understanding that two antagonists might well feel a need for armed forces with which to defend themselves against each other. It then argues that anything beyond the minimum required for self-defence is excessive, and that if both sides could be held down to that minimum, a lot of expense and mutual suspicion would be avoided. If both were subject to comparable constraints, neither would have an excuse for pushing up force levels.

This argument is consistent with a widely held view of the proper role of arms control — putting a 'cap on the arms race' or stopping the 'mad momentum' — according to which success is judged in terms of money not spent, weapons not bought or, better still, weapons decommissioned and force levels reduced. Avoiding an arms race is also felt to be a way of preventing all the passions and suspicions such races generate, since any new increment of military power tends to be justified by reference to the other side's buildup and to the hostile intentions said to be behind it.

There is no close relationship between arms race stability and crisis stability. Two small forces might coexist uneasily, whereas two large forces might develop quite a stable relationship. For this reason, traditional arms control theory never offered any guidelines on the numerical aspect of the nuclear relationship. (The opposite was the case with disarmament theory: to the disarmer every extra weapon represented another step towards disaster; every weapon removed was a blow for peace.) If the concern was for crisis stability in the nuclear age, then once it was possible to ensure a devastating retaliation, extra weapons made very little difference. Meanwhile, up to this point, a state might feel insecure and jumpy. So if levels were allowed to slip below those needed to assure destruction, the resultant uncertainty could well be dangerous. There was no particular worry about 'overkill', the concept that, so long as it was possible to blow everything and everyone up once, all nuclear capabilities beyond that point constituted surplus capacity. Arms controllers did not accept that the level at which 'kill' could be said to have been reached was easy to pinpoint, and feared that a slight 'underkill' might give more scope for miscalculation than a large 'overkill'.

It might be argued that arms race stability is more important than crisis stability, in that arms races generate the crises. However, not only is the proposition that 'arms races always end in wars' (or even 'nearly always') unsupportable by reference to historical evidence, it is also the case that crises or wars can develop for reasons quite unconnected with arms races. If anything, it might be that successful crisis stability should in practice encourage arms race stability, in that the former, if effective, should remove the prospect of gaining exactly the sort of decisive advantage that is said to stimulate arms racing. The existence of arms racing *with* crisis stability suggests we are dealing with a more complex phenomenon than the rhetoric usually suggests. Certainly, the tension between crisis stability and arms race stability is a real one, and its influence will be seen in later chapters.

Moreover, to describe an arms relationship in terms of a race might be a crude oversimplification. It assumes that each move is best explained by reference to an actual, or just potential, move by the adversary. Yet any analysis of decision-making in this area soon reveals a multitude of influences, including the overall economic situation, other demands on the budget, the political dispositions of the policy-makers, bureaucratic interests, the types of weapon available, traditional forms of organization and the lobbying of manufacturers — as well as the judgments of intelligence agencies. Furthermore, even if all these influences cancel each other out, two adversaries are never strategically symmetrical. Armed forces reflect location, terrain and demography, as well as the complex of political relationships in which particular countries find themselves.

All this suggests that in practice the diagnosis of an 'arms race' may be faulty, or true only at such a general level that it is impossible to offer a useful definition of what would constitute arms race stability. A useful definition would be one that could form the basis of a negotiating exercise, for, unlike crisis stability, arms race stability must be agreed by means of negotiations.

In Chapter 4, some of the problems connected with applying arms race stability in practice will be discussed. The concept has had to be reduced to more manageable forms, such as 'parity' or 'sufficiency'. As already indicated, there is room for doubt as to whether we have suffered gross arms race *instability* over the past decades. Military spending in East and West has fluctuated rather than risen steadily; by many quantitative measures, levels have gone down, although qualitatively they have gone up. It would be foolish to deny that weapons are designed with those of the adversary in mind, but there are still many other factors at work. The great surges in military activity have not been the result of a self-generating arms race but of a deterioration in overall political relations.

The negotiations designed to achieve arms race stability have only had a limited success. The most notable outcome of all the negotiating activity of the past three decades has been the channelling of arms competition rather than the ending of it altogether. Thus, there have been agreements which prevent nuclear testing anywhere but underground; but it has been still able to continue underground. There have been agreements not to put nuclear weapons in space, in Antarctica, in Latin America or on the sea-bed; but they can still be developed on the territory of the superpowers and their allies, and in the oceans. The objective of the 1970 nuclear Non-Proliferation Treaty was not to 'roll back' the number of declared nuclear powers, but to hold the number at five. Even in talks on strategic arms, capping one area of weapon development sometimes seems merely to encourage another, which may itself be necessary to create a favourable domestic climate for an agreement.

A concern with arms race stability has therefore encouraged active negotiations, but their record is less than impressive. Meanwhile, a concern with crisis stability suggests little need for active negotiations. Before writing negotiations off, however, one needs to consider the other purposes that they might serve.

3
THE POLITICAL CONTEXT

This chapter will consider the various political objectives that might be met by arms control: the improvement of East-West relations by throwing the arms race into reverse; the exertion of leverage over the Soviet Union; the reinforcement of the established security framework; or the reassurance of public opinion. The very act of negotiation is a substantial political statement. It is generally taken to offer a more wholesome prospect for East-West relations than continued tension, harsh rhetoric and an accelerating arms race. A readiness to engage in arms control demonstrates a commitment to a less belligerent approach. In the 1980s, a large and active anti-nuclear movement provided just the incentive to make such a demonstration.

Is this reassuring impression actually justified? If the arms race were the key to East-West relations, arms control would be the most obvious remedy for international tension. It is widely believed that this is in fact the case, but the arms race on its own provides an inadequate explanation for the course of East-West relations. It is true that major armaments programmes can cause great consternation on the other side, encouraging suspicion of intentions as well as stimulating countermeasures. However, the conflicts which led to postwar rearmament were genuine. When tensions began to ease in the late 1960s, they did so not because of curbs on the arms race but because of the resolution of political differences over Berlin and Europe's postwar boundaries. Similarly, the detente of the 1970s became unstuck for reasons that had little to do with an arms race. The two main factors were Soviet hostility

The political context

to pressure on human rights and American hostility to Soviet adventurism in the Third World. Arms control negotiations patently failed to stop the political rot. As relations worsened, the negotiations became more difficult; arms control might actually have accelerated the decline. The two sides became mutually suspicious, and every negotiating detail was scrutinized for hints of duplicity. Low-level issues became elevated to matters for top-level summitry and provided a steady source of irritation in East-West relations. A deteriorating political climate rendered the negotiating problems even more intractable, which in turn led to a further deterioration in political relations, and so on.

Linkage

Instead of attempting to ease East-West relations by reversing the arms race, an alternative approach is to improve matters by ensuring that the Soviet Union is encouraged to adopt a more 'responsible' international stance. This objective appears to lie behind the concept of 'linkage'. There is, as we have seen, an unavoidable linkage between the overall political relationship and arms control, but this is not the same as adopting a deliberate policy of 'linkage'. Such a policy tempted the Reagan administration early in the 1980s but has now been dropped. It promised progress in arms control only on condition that the Soviet Union refrained from acting against US global interests. This approach implied that arms control agreements were not functional reflections of a coincidence of strategic interests, but essentially involved concessions to the Soviet Union.

Linkage could only work if this were the case. But, of course, the United States would not deliberately negotiate unequal treaties in order to gain political advantage in another context. Such treaties would not pass domestic scrutiny. Certainly the Soviet Union did not think that it had been so uniquely favoured in arms control negotiations that it was obliged to modify its international behaviour. Furthermore, even had it done so, there was no guarantee that a quiet interlude in international affairs, suggestive of more 'responsible' Soviet behaviour and so justifying the passage of a new treaty, might not be ended by a sudden crisis and a bout of Soviet activism. Arms control must operate over the long term, and be justified on its own merits.

The idea of linkage reflected a distinctive feature of the US-Soviet relationship: the two countries have few trading or cultural links, and are not, in any real sense, close neighbours. They tend to judge the state of their relationship by reference to the overall military balance, especially the nuclear balance, and the extent to which they or their allies seem to be in conflict around the globe. So the linkage is not surprising. The regulation of armaments is therefore a more natural way to reflect and condition the overall state of US-Soviet relations than is the case with broader East-West relations. In the relationship between Eastern and Western Europe, non-military factors are much more important, while the relevant military factors are much more complex.

European security remains a critical interest of the USA, yet because of Europe's relative stability, the dynamic in US-Soviet relations has tended to be provided by points of conflict outside the European continent — Southwest Asia, the Middle East, Central America. Here matters are much more fluid. This helps to explain the interest in the United States in linkage, which is used as a means of signalling views on the totality of Soviet behaviour. What this suggests again is not so much that arms control can be used to shape the US-Soviet relationship, but that the reverse is true: arms control will unavoidably reflect the state of the relationship.

Conservation

Linkage makes little sense when applied to Europe, where arms control policies are still conditioned by the overall state of superpower relations, but the politics are far less fluid. The pressures are to conserve and reinforce a well-established status quo, for there is little developing politically to which it is necessary to respond. The West European relationship with Eastern Europe is much deeper than that of the United States with the Soviet Union. West European governments view the Soviet Union as an uncomfortable neighbour with whom it is necessary to reach some sort of modus vivendi.

The political context

In Europe the position adopted by NATO in the late 1960s — to combine detente with defence — is still taken to be the most prudent, whatever the Soviet Union might be getting up to away from the European continent. Detente has meant relief from periodic crises, such as that over Berlin, more contacts at all levels and more trade. The role of arms control has been seen to be one of supporting the established framework of European security; maintaining the cohesion of the Alliance; ensuring that the United States remains committed to the defence of Europe and so balances Soviet military power; and maintaining a reasonable level of communication with the East in order to avoid unnecessary confrontation.

In terms of priorities, the need to sustain the Alliance and the US commitment to Europe has taken precedence over the relationship with the East. Arms control reflects this. There is not only a reluctance to make concessions that might, for example, undermine the US nuclear guarantee or split other members of the Alliance off from one another, but also an unwillingness to move from positions which have been laboriously established in intra-alliance discussions.

The dominant role of the United States within the Alliance means that American views are accorded the most weight. The fact that these views are conditioned by the distinctive nature of the US-Soviet relationship provides an unavoidable source of strain within NATO. The tension is not necessarily between a dove-ish Europe and a hawkish United States, but between a Europe more attached to the status quo and a United States more interested in change, between political management and reform.

Thus, during the Carter administration, there was anxiety in Europe that the determination to reach some SALT agreement might overlook the interests of the allies if, for example, it resulted in restrictive provisions on the transfer of cruise-missile technology. Indeed, up to the later 1970s it was generally believed in Washington that it was the Europeans who were most dubious about arms control. All this illustrates the extent to which the Europeans have sought to use the arms control process to reinforce the established security arrangements, against challenges from both the left and the right, rather than as an agent of change.

The political context

Reassurance

In recent years, the challenge has come largely from the left. Accordingly, NATO governments have often been at their most keen as advocates of arms control when they have wanted to use it as a means of steadying domestic political debate. One obvious example of this is the desire to head off pressure for unilateral reductions in capabilities. A powerful argument against those seeking unilateral cuts (in the hope that they will be reciprocated) is to point to the possibility of the same result being obtained through the less risky route of negotiations. A major motive for entering into the mutual force reduction talks (MBFR) in Vienna in the early 1970s was to head off Congressional demands for substantial cuts in US forces based in Europe. Similarly, the arms control proposal attached to the NATO decision in 1979 to modernize intermediate nuclear forces (INF) stemmed as much from a need to allay West European anxieties about this programme as out of any desire to make some deal with the Russians.

The objectives of arms control are rarely openly expressed in terms of fending off domestic opposition, maintaining force levels, easing the way for new programmes or forging Alliance solidarity; indeed, true believers might see such aims as the negation of arms control. Yet these objectives, if negative, are often quite real to the governments involved. The fact that so little has changed over the past decade may be a source more of satisfaction than of regret to those actually engaged in many of the key negotiations.

Consequently, the value of arms control to governments often lies in the reassuring spectacle of negotiation, rather than in any concrete achievements. But what sort of reassurance can be provided if East-West relations fail to improve and the negotiations fail to reach positive conclusions? A dialogue that takes the form of exchanges of incompatible positions and platitudes does not inspire confidence. A failure to achieve results may provoke cynicism rather than outrage, but it will certainly make the enterprise less useful to governments seeking to resist domestic pressure for more radical changes. Whereas the MBFR talks played an important role in deflating Congressional pressure for troop reductions in the early 1970s, the continuing talks were virtually irrelevant when there was a resurgence of pressure a decade later. The public relations aspect of arms control negotiations does not have a long shelf-life.

In the circumstances of the first half of the 1980s, open scepticism or hostility towards arms control became something of a political liability. It implied rejecting the path of reconciliation and a preference for rearmament. Governments therefore enthused about arms control and were anxious to be seen to be putting forward attractive proposals. Yet, if anything, this enthusiasm made agreements even more difficult to obtain. The attractiveness of proposals was judged primarily in terms of the impression they made on public opinion rather than by the effect on the other side. Since the issue of accepting or refusing US cruise and *Pershing* missiles was a source of great controversy in Western Europe, both the United States and the Soviet Union sought to influence the European debate by means of arms control proposals. This competitive bidding in public made it very difficult to take the negotiations themselves seriously. The sort of compromises needed to achieve actual agreements have to be undertaken by consenting adults in private concentrating on practical measures. Announcing positions that suggest enormous idealism and peaceful intent but address few of the concerns of the other side do not move negotiations along. Once a negotiating position has been made public it can be extremely difficult to move away from it without provoking charges from political opponents of succumbing to pressure or of compromising basic principles. All that one can hope is that in the effort to *appear* reasonable in the negotiations, governments will actually *be* reasonable.

Furthermore, any discussion of arms control tends to lead on to visions of a better world with fewer arms and less tension. It is not necessary to be wholly cynical about these visions. Whatever the doubts about the wisdom of President Reagan's Strategic Defence Initiative, unveiled in his televised speech of March 1983, there is no doubting the sincerity of his belief that this is our best hope for rendering nuclear weapons 'impotent and obsolete'. Nor need we doubt Mr Gorbachev's sincerity when he announced, on 15 January 1986, a schedule for the complete elimination of nuclear weapons by the year 2000. However, the formidable issues of both principle and practice raised by such schemes make it difficult for professional diplomats and specialists to take them seriously. They always seize on the small print rather than the large headlines, the

The political context

detail relevant to negotiations in progress rather than the public relations hyperbole. The public language of arms control is reformist; the private language, managerial. If the public language takes precedence, the private assumption may well be that the other side is not serious about reaching agreements.

4
PARITY AND SUFFICIENCY

The analysis thus far suggests that the political motives behind arms control initiatives are often more important to those making them than the strategic benefits likely to accrue from successful negotiations, and that this may in part derive from the confusion over what the strategic goals of arms control should be. This chapter will demonstrate that, as a result of the combination of a political need for an arms control process and a confusion over goals, the goals have come to be shaped by the process itself. At the very least, the process has encouraged concern with arms race stability in preference to crisis stability.

Parity

This preference was especially evident in the 1970s, as arms control came to be dominated by a drive towards a visible equality — or 'parity' — in the most important measurements of military power. The straightforward notion of parity, which has a resonance in Western culture that gives it immediate appeal, deals with military power at a point at which it can be counted, and can accordingly be justified as a means of achieving arms race stability. Both sides can claim that they are second to none.

As a strategic concept, parity presumes that, whatever their strict military meaning, disparities in capabilities that attract the notice of citizens, allies, adversaries and other interested parties affect the credibility of, and confidence in, a deterrent posture. If, *but only if*, these perceptions truly have an unsettling effect on international security, then a confirmation of parity might have a calming effect by stabilizing perceptions.

It is, unfortunately, difficult to stabilize perceptions, because what is being perceived is subject to change. During the 1970s the weapon systems at the centre of the Strategic Arms Limitation Talks (SALT) — ICBMs, SLBMs and bombers — were straightforward to count and were possessed in broadly similar quantities on either side. But military technology was advancing rapidly and there were growing variations in force structures. The less comparable the two force structures, the more the arguments on the problems of measurement. Arms control became an accounting procedure in which the military assets of the two sides had to be codified in some mutually accepted form. As with all accountancy, there were difficult questions over what to include and exclude on either side of the ledger, and what categories different items were to be placed under; but unlike other accountancy, there was no common currency with which to evaluate the various assets.

Factors that shape force-effectiveness are quite distinct from those that shape public opinion. Public opinion can be influenced by the choice of measure (delivery vehicles, warheads, throw-weight, vulnerability, accuracy, reliability, range). According to one measure, the Soviet Union is well in the lead; but take another and the USA surges ahead. So moving from one to another can make the strategic balance tilt alarmingly or seem comfortably settled. Introducing the issue of the number and proximity of enemies (as the Soviet Union would like to do via the concept of 'equal security', for it must face Britain, France and China as well as the United States) complicates matters further. It is therefore not surprising that, rather than search for an independent yardstick by which to evaluate strategic forces, the two superpowers searched in SALT for a formula to show that existing or planned forces were, to all intents and purposes, already equivalent. Since negotiations usually proceed on the basis of a quid pro quo, which makes unequal concessions unacceptable, it seemed that parity had to exist already before it could be created.

Thus arms control turned into a form of creative accounting in which liberties were taken in evaluating the various systems in order to balance the books. The respective national auditors (to sustain the metaphor), who tended to adopt accounting rules based far more on traditional security interests when evaluating actual or prospective agreements, became unhappy. The process encouraged the tabulation of strategic credits and debits. Even though a SALT II agreement full of ceilings and sub-ceilings was reached in June 1979, it aroused little enthusiasm. It provided few brakes on developments believed to be dangerous, yet the arduous and microscopic examination of the military balance had generated immense arguments within the United States on how to measure strategic power, and had turned minor issues into matters of fundamental policy.

Once the attempt was made to establish parity in one area of arms competition, the process became difficult to stop. Military activity could always be redirected, and symmetry at one level made asymmetries lower down the line seem more important. Arms control was forced to become expansionist, embracing more and more types of weapon so as to establish a comprehensive ledger, with every weapon accounted for and in its place. SALT I, which was signed in May 1972, was conceived with reference to ABMs; in its first phases it included ICBMs and SLBMs; by 1974, bombers were involved; by 1976, cruise missiles had arrived and systems based in the European theatre were implicated; in 1980, preliminary discussion began on long-range theatre nuclear systems; then, during the 1980s, attention moved on to battlefield nuclear systems, and the issue of ABMs was reopened!

Despite the fact that SALT neither clarified the strategic balance nor eased political relations, parity came to be embraced as a guiding principle for all East-West arms control. To quote Chancellor Schmidt of West Germany in his famous 1977 Alastair Buchan Memorial Lecture, 'No one can deny that the principle of parity is a sensible one. However, its fulfilment must be the aim of all arms-limitation and arms-control negotiations and it must apply to all categories of weapons.'

Sufficiency

An alternative approach is based on the concept of 'sufficiency'. Rather than let the adversary set the standards for force levels, and then simply match them through either arms control or armament, forces should be geared purely to meet one's own

Parity and sufficiency

needs. In one sense this idea is unexceptionable. It is wasteful to purchase forces in excess of those absolutely necessary, and dangerous to bargain away those vital to security. In any serious bargaining in a negotiation, a sense of sufficiency helps to distinguish the dispensable from the essential.

Unfortunately, many of the familiar problems with parity recur with sufficiency. Without a clear and agreed identification of the critical elements of military power, the definition of sufficiency becomes subjective and vulnerable to manipulation. Nevertheless, it is at least more useful to start with the question of sufficiency. It draws attention to the extent to which force levels are determined by factors other than the nature of the adversary: for example, the need to reassure allies, to deal with particular geographical vulnerabilities, to live within a budget and encourage new technologies, or simply to reflect long-established military traditions and prejudices.

In addition, it is important to note that even when forces are geared to those of the adversary, they are not necessarily configured in the form of a mirror-image; they may be adapted to protect against or exploit particular developments in the opposing force structure. New defences on one side may well call for improved offences on the other. Highly accurate missiles may encourage a move towards greater mobility, dispersion or concealment. In battle, the interactions between forces are much more complex than those suggested by military balances, in which tanks are always ranged against tanks, aircraft against aircraft and troops against troops, as if they were all fighting separate battles. NATO often points out that it has decided to respond with nuclear forces to a Warsaw Pact advantage in conventional forces, rather than simply go to the expense of matching the Warsaw Pact divisions.

In arms control terms, these sorts of complex interaction could in principle be catered for by 'cross-trading', whereby a concession in one area would be made in return for a concession in a quite different but nevertheless related area. Thus, in the talks on mutual force reductions in Europe in the mid-1970s, NATO offered to reduce its battlefield nuclear systems in return for reductions in the Warsaw Pact tanks that they were designed to confront. However, there have been few offers of a similar nature made since, and many in NATO were unhappy with this example. More frequently, one concession will be offered in return for another in a wholly unrelated area, as part of the overall bargaining process. This is an argument for the two sides to meet at the highest level to review the whole of the arms control process so as to provide the maximum amount of bargaining flexibility, but it has little to do with notions of sufficiency. When it comes to both designing and marketing proposals and agreements, parity is much more comprehensible and powerful.

Sufficiency, then, may serve as a better guide to overall security objectives than parity, and it may help work out priorities for arms control, but it is not necessarily a more convenient organizing principle for the negotiations. However unfortunate, the practice of arms control over the past two decades has propelled consideration of parity to the fore. Partly but not wholly because of this, the way in which strategic relationships are perceived has become a matter of some importance. The perceptions of others have become one more criterion by which sufficiency is judged.

Rather than reject parity out of hand, therefore, a more helpful approach may be to outline the limits of its application. This concept came to be applied to strategic forces because of a widespread view that force levels here had long passed the point at which traditional military criteria were relevant. Furthermore, the systems involved could be easily counted and it was possible to conduct the count in such a way as to show that the two forces were more or less equal. The problems set in when this judgment was not accepted, and military criteria were deemed to be as relevant as ever. The attempt was made to integrate these criteria with the essentially political approach of parity. As already noted, however, the search for a measure of military effectiveness that has some strategic meaning and is also suitable for negotiating purposes has proved difficult.

The attempt has encouraged ways of measuring that are enormously complex and go well beyond perceptions. If the concern is with force effectiveness, questions of compliance are raised in an acute form. By contrast, if the concern is with perceptions, then those systems hidden from view become irrelevant. This suggests that if parity is to succeed, it must be possible — and safe — to use the weapons to make broad political statements about the relationship between the two sides without getting too bound up with questions concerning the military worth of the systems.

Parity and sufficiency

Two more conditions would also seem to be important. First, the relevant forces must lend themselves to the political statement that it is desired to make. It is no good attempting to make a point about equality when the two force structures are patently unequal according to *all* possible measures. Second, the political statement must be kept relatively simple. Something may be said about the US-Soviet relationship by looking at the strategic forces of both sides. Nuclear weapons based in Europe, however, are relevant not only to the US-Soviet relationship, but also to the US relationship with its own allies. Making a statement through arms control about one of these relationships can come only at the expense of the other.

To summarize, parity can be achieved only in circumstances in which classical military criteria are acknowledged to have become less relevant than political criteria in shaping force structures; the force structures nonetheless lend themselves to conveying the appropriate political message; and the political message itself is simple. To take this analysis further, we can now move on to consider the various negotiations.

5
STRATEGIC ARMS CONTROL

The concept of crisis stability was developed largely in relation to strategic arms — the long-range nuclear weapons with which the superpowers threaten each other's homeland. Instability would result from the threat of a 'break-out' from the constraints of mutual assured destruction. If MAD were no longer assured, one side might be tempted to do something rash.

Throughout the 1960s there was little doubt as to which new system threatened a break-out. An effective ballistic-missile defence might allow one side to protect itself against a retaliatory attack and so threaten the other with impunity. The Americans took this essentially paradoxical notion — that defensive measures were destabilizing — far more seriously than the Russians. The Soviet Union saw the development of effective defence as a natural and proper thing to do, but they eventually came to accept the American logic, recognizing just how difficult it was, in practice, to identify, track and intercept an incoming attack. Every development in the defence seemed to be trumped by one in the offence, such as decoys or the splitting up of individual warheads.

In early 1967 the Americans proposed superpower discussions to forestall a new round in the arms race. This was the genesis of SALT, but it took until November 1969 for negotiations actually to begin. Because of the evident failings of ABMs in the face of new offensive technologies, the conditions were ripe for a negotiated agreement. This came in 1972 with the ABM treaty, which is now considered the most important achievement of modern arms control, in that it addressed the original concern about crisis stability.

The treaty limited ABMs to 200 apiece, with 100 to protect the National Command Authority (Moscow or Washington) and another 100 to protect an ICBM field. In 1974 the number was further reduced to 100 ABMs. The Soviet system protecting Moscow never went beyond 64 interceptors; the USA mothballed its own ABM system, which had been designed to defend the *Minuteman* ICBM silos at Grand Forks.

Now that there was no prospect of an effective defence, the only remaining source of instability was a true first-strike capability that could destroy the other side's means of retaliation in a surprise attack. SSBNs roaming the oceans ruled out such a capability.

Nevertheless, the development that demonstrated most dramatically the futility of ABMs — the splitting up of the individual warheads on missiles (MIRVs) — soon came to haunt the negotiations. Placing a number of warheads on single launchers (if combined with sufficient accuracy) made it possible for one ICBM force to eliminate another of a broadly similar size and have a large number of warheads left in reserve. (Attacks against the enemy's military capabilities are known as 'counterforce'.) MIRVs were not perceived as a problem until they were virtually ready for deployment — in the *Minuteman* III ICBM and the *Poseidon* SLBM — by the United States. Then the majority view in Washington was that this was an American advantage, not to be given up without some spectacular concession from the other side. If MIRVs had been seen as a problem early on, controls might have been established; but recognition came late. Anxiety really mounted only when the Soviet Union developed its own MIRVs. Because of its advantage both in ICBM quantity and in throw-weight, the Soviet Union was able to fit large numbers of accurate warheads and realize the full counterforce potential of MIRVing.

The United States sought controls on MIRVing in SALT II. Although some limits were agreed, these were not enough to deny the Soviet Union a substantial counterforce capability, and the failure to achieve such a constraint was one of the chief factors that undermined SALT's reputation in the United States. American proposals in the current Strategic Arms Reductions Talks (START) still place a lot of emphasis on reducing the number of the largest ten-warhead Soviet ICBMs (the 308 SS-18s).

Strategic arms control

Another technological development that proved to be unsettling and which was not effectively curtailed was the cruise missile. The concept was not new (the V1s that dropped on London in 1944 were the first cruise missiles), but a series of incremental advances in propulsion, warhead design and guidance had combined to produce a highly versatile and efficient system. Initially the Soviet Union had the advantage — an early generation of cumbersome and inaccurate cruise missiles, which the Americans unsuccessfully attempted to include in the early stages of SALT. It was a lost opportunity. As the United States began to consider a variety of cruise missile schemes in the later 1970s, the USSR became the *demandeur* for constraints. Again, the achievement was limited: some restrictions on the numbers of aircraft able to carry these missiles and the number of missiles on each aircraft, but not enough to prevent substantial proliferation. Furthermore, the tenuous constraints on ground- and sea-launched cruise missiles embodied in the Protocol of SALT II did not survive the non-ratification of the treaty.

In these two cases technological development dramatically multiplied the number of offensive weapons, and made them far more accurate than their predecessors. The net result was a remarkable increase in the number of land-based targets that could be successfully destroyed in a first strike, supposing that everything worked as it should.

Even so, the continuing invulnerability of nuclear submarines means that the early, essentially stable, relationship still holds. But this has not stopped a mass of speculation on the possible dangers to the United States if its land-based missiles were caught on the ground in a surprise attack. With only inaccurate submarine-based missiles left, the President could only respond to an attack against military targets with one directed against cities. Because he might be reluctant to authorize such escalation, deterrence would be weakened. Such reasoning ignores the great uncertainties connected with an attack targeted solely against military installations. Even if it were successful, it would cause massive civilian casualties that could well lead to an equally massive American response (and what Soviet leader would dare to assume it would not!). Nor would a US President, deprived of his ICBMs, be without alternative means of attacking Soviet military targets, including some highly accurate warheads on submarine-launched missiles.

Strategic arms control

The new weapons made possible new offensive tactics in the event of deterrence failing, but they did not markedly affect the political leaders' assessment of the risks. Although there was loose talk at the time of the SALT II ratification debate of an emerging 'window of opportunity' which was developing for the Soviet Union as a result of its comparative advantage in counterforce capabilities, this window never seemed to open very wide and was officially declared closed in 1983 by the Scowcroft Commission in the United States.

This bipartisan commission had been established in order to sort out the mess that the Reagan administration was getting itself into in its attempt to organize a military response to the counterforce problem. The MX ICBM was a legacy from the Carter administration (in fact its origins can be traced back to the 1960s). It could carry ten powerful and accurate warheads, but the problem was how to protect it from powerful and accurate Soviet warheads. A large number of schemes involving mobility were examined, but they all floundered on a variety of technical, environmental or economic grounds. The Scowcroft Commission could think of no better answer than to put the new ICBMs in old *Minuteman* silos, and declare the problem of their vulnerability to be not as great as had previously been assumed!

New doctrines

The sense of instability associated with MIRVs arose as much from the revision in doctrine that they stimulated as from the actual proliferation in warheads. Over the 1970s the remarkable consensus supporting the conceptual framework of mutual assured destruction, with which the decade began, was eroded. The theory could provide no explanation for the military development of the decade, from MIRVs to cruise missiles; it appeared to be of slight interest to the Soviet Union; and it could provide no convincing answer to the strategic question of what should happen if deterrence failed — would a suicidal and pointless attack on cities be the only option?

As the King MAD died, no new king arrived to be proclaimed in his place. Nor has one emerged yet, though there are plenty of aspirants and pretenders, whose claims tend to revolve around the possibilities for selective targeting or concepts of escalation dominance or, more recently, defence domination. The problem in attempting to establish an alternative is that those on offer have failed either to break the association between any nuclear use and utter catastrophe or to demonstrate that mutual assured destruction is just one option among many rather than an ever-present fact of international life. Therefore, although it is not just the collapse of a conceptual framework that has left arms control floundering, a necessary condition for its revival will have to be an attempt to reconstruct such a framework to guide initiatives and assess proposals.

The Reagan administration began in 1981 with an attempt to build on the countervailing strategy of the Carter administration to construct a set of nuclear capabilities that would allow a variety of types of nuclear operation over an extended period. This strategy was justified largely by the belief that the Soviet Union already had a philosophy of prolonged nuclear war and the capabilities to implement it. Although this approach still guides much force planning and strategic targeting, it has not been found easy to justify it in public, and many critical difficulties have emerged, especially in the area of command and control. There is also some evidence that the Soviet Union has been losing confidence in its capacity to wage nuclear war as an extension of a traditional military campaign. The administration has now moved to a philosophy which places less emphasis on nuclear deterrence. Certainly the deep cuts envisaged in its most recent START proposals would reduce its ability to implement the countervailing strategy.

More seriously, the Strategic Defence Initiative has been justified in terms of a desire to move from an offence-dominated to a defence-dominated world, from mutual assured destruction to mutual assured survival. SDI is based on an optimism with regard to the prospects for breakthroughs in defensive technologies, especially those based in space. It has also acknowledged that any transition to the new strategic order will have to be negotiated. This is because of the need to remove the current restrictions on defences embodied in the 1972 ABM treaty, and because it is recognized that a situation in which there is a mix of offensive and defensive systems could be highly unstable. President Reagan has even offered to transfer some of the relevant technology to the Soviet Union, once it has been developed.

Administration spokesmen have argued that as SDI gathers pace, the Soviet Union will see the futility of persevering with ICBMs and be prepared to negotiate restrictions. There is, however, no reason why this should be so. More likely, the uncertainty over strategic defences will make it difficult for the Soviet Union to agree to limits on its offensive forces. In the short term, therefore, the new philosophy provides no conceptual basis for arms control. Limitations on offensive forces will require the maintenance and even reinforcement of the ABM treaty.

Nor does this philosophy promise to set the terms for strategic arms control over the long term. The proposed new defences would not be ready until the next century. The Strategic Defence Initiative will be sustained for the next few years by the commitment of the President, but the conceptual difficulties posed by the introduction of defences that are unlikely to protect the population as a whole, the lack of comparable defences against bombers and cruise missiles, the availability of countermeasures and the sheer technological ambition and cost all cast doubt on the extent to which SDI will shape arms control in the future.

The doubts over the durability, wisdom and morality of deterrence that inform the SDI have helped to create the climate for an alternative approach which is also being followed by the Reagan administration and the Soviet Union. This seeks deep cuts in strategic arsenals. We have noted that traditional arms control theory has little to say about the desirable numerical level at which a nuclear balance can be sustained, while recent arms control practice has been preoccupied with achieving parity. Both hawks and doves have complained that parity at high levels merely consolidates the status quo and they have therefore demanded something more radical. Their concern has been reflected in the 'deep cuts' philosophy (which can be traced back to an offer made by President Carter in March 1977).

It is clear that whatever the strategic instabilities that might emerge at much lower numbers (less than a tenth of current arsenals), not even a proposed 50 per cent cut makes much difference to the basic condition of mutual assured destruction. There are two marginal advantages which might justify such a reduction. First, command and control problems should be eased with fewer systems. Second, there ought to be some financial savings. The main advantage, though, which reflects the way nuclear weapons have come to be viewed, is that large-scale reductions would be seen to be politically important.

The concept of parity has encouraged the view that the state of the nuclear balance provides a political statement on the relationship between the superpowers, so a cut would imply that things are getting better. Since such an agreement will not be achieved until political relations have improved, the perception created would be correct. The important point is that neither the strategic nor the political significance of such a move should be exaggerated. Stability in the nuclear age depends on the nuclear arsenals appearing unambiguously horrible. Reducing the pace and the breadth of technological innovation or the overall numbers of the weapons even to a low level is not going to make nuclear war less horrible.

Nevertheless, although deep cuts will not take us out of the age of nuclear deterrence, the readiness to contemplate such cuts does reflect a certain loss of confidence in nuclear strategy. As discussed earlier, a force structure is most likely to be shaped according to political criteria if military criteria are seen to be significantly less important. In this way, arms control may be reflecting (but not creating) an important trend in strategic thinking which many Western (and Eastern) strategists may deplore, but cannot ignore. The difficulty in devising believable war-plans for nuclear weapons has undermined the view that deterrence depends only on the credibility of nuclear threats. It is now recognized that the quality of conventional forces is very relevant to the deterrent equation. In addition, it is being argued increasingly that what deters is not so much the actual *threat* to use nuclear weapons in response to aggression as the recognition that, even if it would be irrational to implement such a threat, so long as nuclear weapons exist in significant numbers there is always the chance that they will be used, in the context of a major war.

Thus, while trends in strategic thinking have created the intellectual climate for deep cuts, they have not yet done so for the complete elimination of nuclear weapons, despite the support given by both superpowers to this radical step. Even if such an idea did not face so many technical and political obstacles, there remain profound intellectual objections. These have been voiced firmly to

President Reagan by his West European allies. Unlike the United States, which is only vulnerable to nuclear attack, Western Europe is also vulnerable to conventional attack. Without the possibility that nuclear weapons might just be detonated, aggression could become easier to contemplate. There are, of course, other means of preventing aggression, through conventional forces or stronger international organizations or simply a process of political reconciliation. In time, development along these lines may create conditions in which further large-scale steps might be contemplated. Such conditions are not yet close.

Prospects

In the flurry of activity preceding the Reagan/Gorbachev summit of November 1985, the two sides moved closer together on the question of deep cuts. They were now talking about a limit of somewhere between 1,600 and 1,800 launchers, and a ceiling of 6,000 strategic warheads, with no more than 50 to 60 per cent of missile warheads to be on land-based systems. The two critical differences were, first, that the United States wanted to keep the ceilings for bombers and missiles separate (thus denying the Soviet Union full compensation for the US advantage in bombers), while the Soviet Union wished to integrate the two. Second, and more important, the US count included only longer-range systems, while the Soviet Union counted all systems that could hit its territory including those based in Europe. Unless this last demand were negotiable, there could be no agreement.

In one very simple sense the future of the current negotiating effort is still bound up with SDI. The Soviet Union is unlikely to agree to major reductions or even limitations in its offensive arms without some confidence that there would be no substantial surge in US defensive capabilities. If the United States wishes to keep open all its options in the defensive area, then the Soviet Union will no doubt wish to do likewise in the offensive area.

However, the formal Soviet position up to the summit — that *all* research in this area should be prohibited — was untenable. Even if the principle had been accepted verification would be impossible. Many of the research programmes currently funded under SDI started well before the President's speech and could be justified under a number of headings, not just 'strategic defence'. If SDI research were abandoned, they could be dispersed around the research community. Nor was the Soviet Union on particularly strong ground with regard to the principle. Both sides have had research programmes of some sort underway since the 1972 treaty was signed. The Soviet argument that there was something special about research designed to put defensive systems in space was not persuasive.

A Soviet position more firmly based on the ABM treaty would be more effective. The treaty was designed to prevent the introduction of new defences. So long as the treaty is in force there can be no serious buildup of US strategic defences. No new arms control is required. The only question is the point along the road from research — through development and testing — to deployment at which a continuing SDI would come up against the barriers imposed by the treaty. This issue has already proved to be controversial. In early October 1985 the United States unveiled an interpretation of the treaty which suggested that it permitted virtually everything other than actual deployment. Under pressure from allies, Secretary of State George Schultz explained that although the permissive interpretation could be justified, the United States was operating, and would continue to operate, with the more restrictive interpretation. Should the research make real progress this issue could easily be revived.

The most logical approach to SDI from the Soviet point of view is therefore to tolerate research but to press the Americans on the boundaries which must not be passed if the ABM treaty is to remain effective. In June 1986, there were indications that the Soviet Union was moving in this direction, linking reductions in ICBMs to a strengthening of the treaty, including an extension of the notice required, before leaving the treaty, from months to years. Many of the allies of the United States, and indeed many within the Reagan administration, would consider such an approach quite reasonable, and would find it difficult to say why it was not. If, then, the Soviet Union is prepared to move away from its absolute insistence on the abandonment of the SDI research programme, and if the USA does not waver in its readiness to stay within the terms of the ABM treaty, this issue could be defused quite rapidly. The natural compromise on SDI is a serious negotiation on what is actually permitted under the terms of the treaty. It should be noted that a negotiation based on the ABM treaty will allow the United States to raise the vexed question of phased-array radar at Krasnayorsk (and, for that matter, the Soviet Union to raise the issue of the new American phased-array radars at Thule in Greenland and Fylingdales in England).

The greatest negotiating challenge remains where it has always been: in reaching an agreement on strategic offensive arms. The pre-summit announcements marked a genuine movement in the position of both sides. However, the Soviet Union clearly found it difficult to build on this movement. When it eventually responded to the American proposals, there was a retreat from 50 per cent cuts. Its new proposal envisaged only 30 per cent, raising the warhead limit to 8,000. No more than 60 per cent of this level could be on a single leg of the strategic triad of bombers, ICBMs and SLBMs. But this revived the American fears of an agreement leaving a Soviet advantage in the more powerful ICBMs. More positively, the Soviet Union no longer included US forward-based systems (though a freeze was still required), it was prepared to tolerate cruise missiles on submarines (but not on surface ships), and had new ideas on verification. The two sides were not hopelessly apart, as President Reagan acknowledged publicly, and it was possible to envisage a framework agreement. Unfortunately, this is an area where the technical details are extremely difficult and might still frustrate the negotiating effort. Will the United States insist on including Soviet *Backfire* bombers in its strategic totals? How will submarine-launched cruise missiles be verified? It was exactly this kind of issue that held up SALT II for so long after Presidents Ford and Brezhnev had reached a framework agreement at Vladivostok in November 1974.

6
INTERMEDIATE NUCLEAR FORCES

In Europe only one of the three conditions discussed at the end of Chapter 4 for the successful pursuit of nuclear parity obtains. Political criteria are generally more important than military criteria in shaping force structures (at least on the NATO side), but the two force structures are hopelessly asymmetrical and offer no natural parity, and the political messages that they convey are extremely complex.

US nuclear forces based in Europe are of three sorts: 'battlefield', which are of a short range and can be used in a combat zone; 'medium-range', which can hit targets behind the front line in Eastern Europe; and 'intermediate', which can hit Soviet territory from European bases. Their basic political purpose is to reassure West Europeans that the United States is prepared to defend them by nuclear means if necessary, and to give an extra degree of deterrence by adding to the risks of escalation following any Soviet aggression. The Europeans have themselves preferred to rely on this threatened escalation, despite the risk of their own destruction, rather than pay the extra cost of a credible conventional defence.

The Soviet Union has consistently argued that the intermediate and any medium-range nuclear forces that can hit its territory deserve to be classed as 'strategic' and treated accordingly. In principle NATO need not object to this classification. However, it would need to insist that Soviet systems threatening Western Europe are also strategic. The Soviet Union likes to present the basic strategic conflict as one between two superpowers, with the

Intermediate nuclear forces

allies in wholly secondary and subordinate roles. NATO in principle at least sees its alliance as a unity.

In practice, the West European governments do consider the European-based systems to have the special significance of coupling the defence of Europe to the American strategic nuclear arsenal. They have always been fearful of a superpower agreement which would remove these systems, and so detach US strategic forces from the defence of Europe. This issue dogged strategic arms talks from the start, and came to the fore when NATO ministers decided in December 1979 to go ahead with a programme to modernize intermediate nuclear forces (then known as Long-Range Theatre Nuclear Forces) by deploying 464 *Tomahawk* cruise missiles and 108 *Pershing* ballistic missiles throughout Europe. This programme was supported by one group who believed that it had to be implemented irrespective of arms control, and another who believed it could be bargained away through arms control so as to secure restraints on Soviet forces facing Europe. All agreed that in order to obtain domestic support for the planned NATO deployment, it was vital to make (or at least to give the appearance of making) a serious effort to come to some sort of agreement on this matter with the Soviet Union.

The mobile Soviet SS-20 missile with its three warheads, which had first attracted attention in 1975, was used by Western leaders to assign responsibility for any arms race to the East. The opportunity to justify the modernization programme by reference to the SS-20 was too good to miss, and the future of the two programmes was seen to be linked. In addition, the search for parity at the central strategic level was focusing attention on asymmetries lower down the line. All this led to the view in 1979 that it was necessary to produce an arms control proposal in parallel with the plans for force modernization.

Up to this point there was no history of a positive West European view on the application of nuclear arms control to the Continent. The British and French had refused to let their own nuclear forces be involved. The European consensus had been that American nuclear systems based on the Continent were too important as a link with the US strategic arsenal and had best not be tampered with. Much of the argument over SALT II was that it might be harmful to European security by failing to constrain Soviet 'theatre' forces while limiting US 'theatre' forces assigned

Intermediate nuclear forces

to NATO. West European governments themselves, therefore, had no tradition of nuclear arms control and had demonstrated no great interest in the content of SALT. Their concern was with the political implications of the challenge to detente represented by the failure of SALT. In addition, the anti-nuclear movement was making them nervous. If the whole nuclear issue could be handled through the mechanisms of traditional diplomacy rather than on the streets, then it could be kept under control. Again, arms control was seen as much as a means to political ends as a way of stabilizing military relations.

INF negotiations

The disposition of nuclear arms in Europe exhibits no symmetry whatsoever in the types of system held by each side, their age, capabilities or numbers. No potential agreement leaps out from the figures (as it does to some extent with strategic arms). This unpromising picture has been made worse by the artificial nature of the INF category, which is illustrated by the fact that there is little agreement even with NATO as to its boundaries. INF is an offshoot of SALT without its own identity. The divorce from negotiations on central strategic systems was always unnatural, given the overlap between the two.

Within the negotiations (discussed in detail in Appendix 3), the loss of the wider context of strategic arms negotiations soon became a major handicap. It threw into relief the specific asymmetries at the theatre level. In terms of NATO doctrine, it undermined the idea of a continuum of deterrence, by separating a theatre from a strategic balance.

The aim was to size up the theatre balance to see where and how the concessions would have to be made to construct an acceptable parity. Out of this effort emerged the basic disagreement that caused the lack of progress at Geneva. Whether one focused narrowly on modern missiles or broadly on missiles and aircraft of all ages, the essential problem was that whereas NATO argued that parity was a good thing but had to be created, the Soviet Union argued that parity was a good thing and existed already — and so had to be preserved.

In principle this dispute ought to have been solved by reference to the evidence. Unfortunately, the difficulty was not how to count but what to count, for both sides disagree on what should and what should not be included in the tally. This is discussed further in Appendix 4.

The United States began by arguing for zero in intermediate missiles, and required Soviet forces in Asia to be eliminated along with those in Europe. The Soviet Union argued for reductions of all systems in the European zone alone. The nearest the two sides came to an agreement was the famous Nitze/Kvitsinsky 'walk in the woods' compromise of July 1982. The basis of that deal, worked out informally between the two chief negotiators, was that the Soviet Union gained the cancellation of *Pershing* and a freeze instead of a reduction in its Far Eastern deployments, while the United States was allowed some 300 cruise missiles in Europe in return for a reduction of SS-20s to 75 (225 warheads).

This was taken as a reasonably clear indication of Soviet priorities, and especially of the relative menace they attached to *Pershing* as against cruise. In 1979, *Pershing* II, a ballistic missile with a name that implied a mere evolution from an existing system, seemed far less controversial than cruise missiles, which were already the subject of great controversy. However, to the Russians there was all the difference between *Pershing* II, which can reach Soviet territory, and *Pershing* I, which cannot. Along with the NATO planners, they viewed *Pershing* as being somewhat more capable than cruise missiles.

Pershing II carries a 10–20 kiloton warhead over 1,000 miles to an accuracy of some 120 feet. Unlike cruise missiles, however, ballistic missiles are not vulnerable to known forms of defence and do not fly at subsonic speeds. Soviet propaganda began to describe *Pershing* as a dire threat to Soviet national security, even as an instrument of first strike, despite the fact that 108 missiles could hardly represent a threat to 2,000 Soviet ICBMs, most of which were well out of range. The real problem was the short flight-time of *Pershing* (seven minutes according to the Soviet Union; twelve minutes according to NATO), which would reduce the warning-time of an imminent attack. Soviet strategists may also have linked *Pershing* to some US concepts of 'decapitation', by which the Central Command would be paralysed in a surprise nuclear attack and so would be unable to assess the situation or get out the orders to its nuclear forces, even if they survived intact. This fear presumed that *Pershing* could reach Moscow; NATO said it could not.

Because the Soviet arguments were considered bogus NATO was unwilling to grant special treatment to *Pershing* in arms control. The 'walk in the woods' deal confirmed a particular Soviet interest in *Pershing*. In rejecting this deal, the US government conceded the greater capability of ballistic as against cruise missiles, and hence its unwillingness to let the USSR have a monopoly of ballistic missiles in Europe.

It was not until late 1985 that the two sides appeared to be moving towards a deal. The move began with Gorbachev's Paris speech of 3 October, in which a confusing and in some ways contradictory set of proposals was presented. In the proposal on strategic offensive arms, Gorbachev included all US forward-based systems, a suggestion that, on its most positive interpretation, might prepare the ground for an integration of START and INF if comparable Soviet systems could also be included; yet he also offered to conduct separate talks with Britain and France; and then said it was still possible to conclude an agreement with the USA along the lines previously proposed at the INF talks, essentially by freezing existing forces. Cruise missiles were banned at one point, frozen somewhere else, and then counted in somewhere else again.

The position here may have reflected a tension between two distinct Soviet views. The traditional view, which had been expressed from the start of SALT in 1969 and had been held throughout the 1970s, was that the United States should accept restrictions on any nuclear system that could attack Soviet territory, but that Soviet systems of comparable range were irrelevant so long as they could not hit US territory. This view was altered during the course of the effort to head off the cruise and *Pershing* deployments. It was no longer possible to pretend that Soviet systems threatening America's allies could be excluded, while those US systems committed to the defence of these allies were to be subjected to severe restraint. In the first half of the 1980s, the Soviet position had moved from arguing that the European balance was irrelevant to the view that it was relevant but was fortunately already in a condition of parity. Only the new US missiles threatened this parity.

In arguing this point, the Soviet Union had attempted to

Intermediate nuclear forces

demonstrate an integral link between the number of Soviet SS-20s and British and French missile numbers. In October Gorbachev took this further by offering direct talks with Britain and France. This offer was rejected immediately by President Mitterrand and by Prime Minister Thatcher shortly afterwards. The Soviet freeze proposal would have linked the number of NATO missiles (American and British and French) with the number of SS-20s facing Western Europe, and in this sense involved a concession, since it allowed for some American role. In its response the United States picked up the Soviet freeze proposal to the extent that it was prepared to limit its own deployments to the 140 launchers to be in place at the end of 1985. Each cruise missile launcher carries four missiles, so the total of 140 launchers was made up of 108 *Pershings* and 32 cruise launchers (or 128 missiles), making a warhead total of 236. The United States, however, wanted the Soviet Union to reduce its SS-20s facing Western Europe to the same number. Proportionate cuts would also be expected in those SS-20s based in the Far East (estimates suggested a cut from 170 to 100 launchers). The United States would retain the right to an equivalent global level but made it clear that it would not match the Far Eastern systems. In total, therefore, the Soviet Union would have some 240 launchers or 720 warheads (with 420 warheads facing Western Europe). The United States wanted the right to alter the mix between *Pershing* and cruise launchers to bring its warhead count in Europe up to an equivalent level. This would be done by cutting the *Pershing* force to around 34 and raising the cruise launcher total to around 100 (400 missiles).

The Soviet Union might have been expected to have mixed feelings on this matter, in that its irritation at the rise in US warheads might have been eased by the decline in *Pershing* numbers. For the Kremlin, though, the main problem with the US proposal was that it cut Soviet Far Eastern deployments (only a freeze had been offered) and provided no compensation for the 160 British and French missiles. One of the features of the Soviet position that intrigued the USA was that a deal on strategic arms was no longer made dependent on progress in INF. The Agreed Statement after the November summit mentioned the possibility of an interim INF agreement, indicating an interest in a quick deal on INF as a means of setting the pace for the other talks.

This impression was confirmed on 15 January 1986, when

Intermediate nuclear forces

Gorbachev made yet another offer. This time, however, there was a major departure from previous positions. Gorbachev was now willing to eliminate all intermediate-range missiles from Europe. This differed from President Reagan's original 'zero option' in two respects: it was confined to Europe and so did not include the Far Eastern SS-20s; and it required that there be no buildup in the British and French nuclear forces.

President Reagan could legitimately see this as a vindication of his 'bargaining chip' philosophy. In the four years from November 1981, when he had proposed his own zero option, the NATO missiles had moved from a controversial plan to reality, and had changed the balance of Soviet incentives. However, for many in the NATO establishment, Gorbachev's zero option confirmed their original misgivings about President Reagan's version. Cruise and *Pershing* were *not* intended to be simply responses to the SS-20, but reflected the special needs of the Alliance. They were concerned that the Soviets now realized they had an opportunity to disrupt Alliance strategy, and that they would in the process be removing a threat to themselves in return for an easing of a threat only to America's allies.

The Americans felt they had no option but to respond positively to Gorbachev's statement. Their initial response was to accept the zero option for Europe, but reject any restrictions on British and French forces and insist on proportionate reductions in the SS-20s facing the Far East. However, the Japanese insisted that what was good enough for America's European allies was good enough for them, and so they wanted to be faced by *zero* SS-20s and not 70. The President accordingly responded to Gorbachev with a recapitulation of his original zero option, applying it globally and not just to Europe. He offered the Soviet Union three routes to this end, including staged reductions, and therefore opened up the possibility of stopping at one of these stages and not quite reaching zero! It is clear that if there is to be any further progress, some understanding will have to be reached on the Soviet Far Eastern forces. The most obvious compromise would be some reduction in their number, but not necessarily as drastic as that required of the SS-20s facing Europe. Given its concern over China, it is hard to see the Soviet Union altogether abandoning its SS-20 force in this area.

What about a possible compromise on Mr Gorbachev's other

condition, requiring no buildup of British and French forces? These forces have been raised in arms control since the early 1970s but they only became prominent in Soviet proposals in the early 1980s, first in constructing a European 'balance' that suited Soviet claims, and then in an attempt to establish a direct link between the British and French forces and the number of SS-20s.

This link was contrived. There is no evidence that either side planned its missile force with reference to this relationship. There were medium- and intermediate-range Soviet missiles facing Western Europe long before there were any British and French missiles. Britain and France insist that their missiles are designed to deter the totality of Soviet systems and not just one component. Other West European countries look to Washington, not London or Paris, for their nuclear guarantees. Even if there is some loose numerical relationship with missiles, there is absolutely none when it comes to long-range aircraft. In any case, the Soviet objective was not to seek reductions in British and French forces, but to use these forces to make a case for excluding American forces from the Continent. Nevertheless, there has always been some sympathy in the West that, at a time when the USSR is being asked to subject its forces to arms control constraints, no such constraints should be imposed on other nuclear powers threatening Soviet territory. Furthermore, improvements planned for the European nuclear forces will greatly increase the number of warheads deployed. The new French M-4 SLBM, for example, has six warheads (although they are not fully independently targetable). The Soviet Union insists that the recent modernization of the British *Polaris* force to carry the Chevaline warhead raises the warhead count from 3 to 6, though this last figure is wrong. (In fact Chevaline involves a reduction to two.) There is no doubt that the replacement of *Polaris* by *Trident* will multiply the number of warheads by a factor of about four. If we are moving to a period of deep reductions in superpower arsenals, then Britain and France will loom larger on the strategic landscape, and a lack of constraint will appear anomalous.

Although the British and French forces are normally considered together, there are important differences in the attitudes and force structures of the two countries that lead to more pressure on London than on Paris. Politically British governments have always been positive about arms control, and have even justified the national nuclear deterrent on the grounds that it provides a voice in great power negotiations — a ticket to the top table. In addition, the nuclear force is controversial domestically, and it does not help if it is identified as a barrier to arms control. France, on the other hand, enjoys a national consensus supporting its *force de frappe* and has always steered clear of arms control. Britain has American missiles and, although *Polaris* is no longer in the US inventory, in the 1990s both countries will have the *Trident* D-5. France's missiles are quite distinct. Lastly, Britain has assigned its forces to NATO and they are targeted along with US forces at Omaha (although quite separate target lists are also maintained). France is not part of NATO's Integrated Military Command and has placed great stress on the autonomy of its nuclear policy.

To head off pressure the British government has argued that although the number of warheads will go up with *Trident*, the Soviet Union has hardly been dragging its feet when it comes to upping warhead numbers. So when *Trident* arrives in the 1990s, the ratio of British to Soviet warheads will be the same as when *Polaris* was introduced in the 1960s. If British submarine-based forces are to be discussed, they should logically come under START, not INF. At any rate, both of these have been bilateral negotiations, and the United States cannot be expected to negotiate on behalf of other sovereign powers. Nor can the Americans be expected to accept that their forces should be reduced to make way for British and French forces.

Despite these objections Britain has not ruled out eventual involvement. Two conditions would have to be satisfied. There would have to be substantial reductions in the superpower offensive forces, and no improvement in Soviet defensive capabilities. The interesting aspect of this second point, of course, is that it puts the British government in line with the Soviet government in arguing the unreality of expecting limitations on offensive arms when there are long-term doubts over the defensive position. It also stresses Britain's stake in the ABM treaty, which makes small nuclear deterrents more credible.

The link with superpower reductions in offensive arms is more surprising. It suggests that Britain could make proportionate reductions to match the superpowers. But Britain could not reduce its four submarines to two, for that would mean long periods when no boat was on station (because of the pattern of patrol times and

Intermediate nuclear forces

long refits). Four SSBNs constitute a minimum deterrent. Consequently Britain lacks a flexible negotiating position.

All that Mr Gorbachev has offered in return for the complete abandonment of the *Polaris* force (when this issue has been raised by the Labour Party) has been the reduction of an equivalent number of Soviet missiles. It is hard to see how even this much could be agreed in the absence of a comprehensive INF agreement, in that without fixed ceilings on all relevant systems it would be impossible either to mark the reduction in Soviet capability or to ensure that it was permanent.

In his 15 January speech Mr Gorbachev was careful to argue for no more than a freeze on warhead numbers. Only a buildup was to be avoided: he did not even preclude some forms of modernization. Britain rejected this approach, in that it would still in effect have forced Britain out of the nuclear business by preventing the acquisition of *Trident*. The government hoped that there was no serious expectation in Moscow that Britain would take any other position and that, should it come to the crunch, the Soviets would not push this issue at the expense of an agreement with the United States. However, Britain may still find itself under pressure to do something to facilitate compromise in this area. For example, it could be suggested that there be bilateral discussions with the Soviet Union — but in the context of the strategic arms talks rather than INF — to produce a UK/USSR agreement that would only come into force in the event of a US/Soviet agreement. It might prove to be sufficient for the Soviet Union to have an agreement on the *principle* that the British forces should be subject in some way to limitations rather than that they be reduced or frozen. It might be possible, for example, to freeze submarine numbers or their operational launch tubes. It might even be possible to agree on a ceiling for UK *Trident* warheads somewhat below the maximum. Such actions would be symbolic but they would make a political point. The point might even have a further use for the government, since it would confer upon the UK forces a domestic and international legitimacy that they currently lack.

The British hope is that the Soviet Union has no great expectations with regard to British and French nuclear weapons, and is only using the issue for bargaining purposes. There are plenty of indications that at the crunch it will withdraw pressure on the European nuclear forces if it can obtain its primary objectives with regard to the American forces by alternative means. The United States has no desire to allow the Soviet Union to establish the principle of Soviet numbers matching a combined British, French and American total.

By the summer of 1986, there were indications that the issue of the European deterrent could be deferred to START. Britain could still come under some pressure in these negotiations. If the two superpowers wish to take these forces into account, Britain is in no position to object. Nor is it in a position to pretend that it has only a slight direct interest in the outcome. For example, if the Soviet Union succeeded in one of its prime objectives — that of preventing the introduction of the *Trident* D-5 — it would have important consequences for Britain, as would any possible amendment of the ABM treaty. It may be that the most fruitful course for Britain to take would be to accept Mr Gorbachev's offer of direct negotiations, but not on the terms in which this was couched. All Britain can really offer is a freeze on SSBN numbers or on missile launch tubes. It might be possible to establish ceilings on warhead numbers in launch tubes with *Trident*, even at numbers slightly lower than currently planned. After all, if the Kremlin already believes that *Polaris* has six warheads, why not freeze that number! But warhead limitations, because of a possibly higher American level, raise verification problems; sealing off some launch tubes (leaving 12 out of 16 for example) might be easier.

As already mentioned, such proposals could be offered in the context of a bilateral London/Moscow agreement which would come into effect together with a Washington/Moscow agreement. It would not involve major reductions in the British force, and in fact would legitimize this force, although there could be no guarantee that France would follow. The result would be that Soviet planners would have an extra increment of predictability and there would be an acceptance of the principle that these forces would not be excluded from an arms control regime. None of this solves the INF problem.

If all this were agreed, it is not inconceivable that the cruise and *Pershings* and the SS-20s would be removed in what would no doubt be claimed as a great victory for arms control. The focus of attention would then be on the medium-range and battlefield nuclear weapons. Without INF, these would take on an increased

Intermediate nuclear forces

importance for NATO, because they would now constitute the US nuclear presence in Europe. There would therefore be greater resistance than before to removing them either in the context of an arms control deal or because of an alliance-wide reappraisal of force structure. This is unfortunate, for in terms of crisis stability battlefield nuclear weapons cause far more problems than the longer-range systems, simply because they are much more likely to be used early in a conflict and cause a premature crossing of the nuclear threshold. Over the past few years, NATO has been steadily reducing its numbers of weapons of this range, in response to doubts over their strategic value and because longer-range systems have been preferred. This process may now be arrested.

Mr Gorbachev, too, has envisaged that these systems could eventually be removed. However, apart from the fact that the loss of all US nuclear weapons from the Continent would lead to all sorts of anxieties in Western Europe, in that nuclear deterrence would be weakened while little was happening to ease the conventional threat, these shorter-range systems are quite unpromising subjects for traditional arms control. There is again an asymmetry: both blocs have similar numbers of nuclear-capable artillery pieces (just over 4,000), but the USSR has some 700 nuclear-capable short-range missiles as against NATO's 100. However, the main problem is that these systems are dual-capable and therefore could not be eliminated without interfering with conventional capabilities. Thus only 1,100 of NATO's 4,000 nuclear-capable artillery pieces have actually been assigned to nuclear roles. Furthermore, given the ease with which these systems can be dispersed and concealed, and the importance of the actual warheads rather than simply the means of their delivery, verification would be difficult. Indeed, if arms control negotiations had been underway in the past, they would probably have been used as an excuse for not undertaking the modest measures of reduction that have been set in train by NATO. Why, it would have been asked, reduce unilaterally when you might bring down Warsaw Pact numbers in a multilateral negotiation? The difficulty in bringing any such negotiation to a conclusion would have kept both NATO and Warsaw Pact numbers up. Here, then, is a case in which hard questions of sufficiency are more useful, and the idea of parity is a diversion.

7
MUTUAL AND BALANCED FORCE REDUCTIONS

If any evidence were needed that arms control talks which have been set in motion for political purposes without a clear basis for agreement can lead to futility and stagnation, it is provided by the MBFR talks. Exploratory talks on Mutual Reductions on Forces and Armaments and Associated Measures in Central Europe (MBFR for short) opened in January 1973, and the negotiations proper began in Vienna on 30 October of the same year. They have yet to reach a conclusion.

Origins

The origins of MBFR arose out of a sense of political, rather than military, problems and opportunities. The difficulty has been that whereas the primary objectives for both sides were met by establishing the negotiations and did not require actual agreement, their secondary objectives have been incompatible.

In 1968, NATO made its first call for the initiation of 'a process leading to mutual force reductions'. A response was eventually forthcoming from the East. On 14 May 1971, at a speech in Tiflis, Brezhnev called for exploratory talks, though it required NATO agreement on a Conference on Security and Cooperation in Europe (CSCE) for the explorations to begin.

All this was part of the deliberate moves at that time towards detente which, though interrupted by the August 1968 Soviet invasion of Czechoslovakia, proceeded apace in the early 1970s:

Mutual and balanced force reductions

first, West Germany concluded a Non-Aggression Treaty with the Soviet Union and normalized relations with Poland in 1970; then came the first SALT agreements and the Four-Power Agreement on Berlin; and the CSCE itself began in Helsinki in 1972. For NATO, force reduction talks provided an opportunity to show its member countries working together for detente, rather than just defence, and to draw East European countries into a dialogue, rather than passing all communications through Moscow.

A second purpose was somewhat less noble. In the second half of the 1960s NATO's position in Europe had begun to decline as France left the Integrated Military Command, Britain reduced its forces slightly, and the United States, preoccupied with Vietnam, reduced its forces substantially. Meanwhile pressure was growing in the United States for further reductions. Senate majority leader Mike Mansfield submitted regular resolutions calling for major troop cuts. The idea of mutual force reductions was put forward to forestall unilateral American cuts by arguing against wasting an opportunity to achieve similar cuts in Soviet forces. The argument succeeded. What is surprising is that Leonid Brezhnev was an accomplice in this attempt. His Tiflis speech calling for negotiations came the day before a critical Senate vote on Mansfield's troop-cut proposals which, presented as an amendment to another bill, would have had the force of law. The Soviet Union lent its assistance because it believed that US forces in Europe were a stabilizing factor and that their withdrawal could leave a vacuum that was likely to be filled by West Germany. Its main objective was to consolidate the political status quo in Europe and thereby Soviet domination of Eastern Europe.

For both sides the immediate objectives were achieved. The domestic pressure for US troop withdrawals subsided, while the Soviet Union got its conference on European security. To the extent that the deal was MBFR for the West in return for CSCE for the East, it turned out to be a mixed blessing for both. Moscow, to its chagrin, saw the CSCE being used by the West, via arguments on human rights, to undermine its legitimacy in Eastern Europe; and NATO has failed to achieve any improvement in its security position.

Mutual and balanced force reductions

Parity and security

In these circumstances, NATO naturally gravitated towards the principle of parity. The slow progress in the negotiations towards this end is recorded in Appendix 5. More significant than the glacial movement is the narrow focus, which diminishes the value of anything that might actually be achieved, and throws into relief the question of the relationship between parity and security.

The principle of parity was accepted early on and firm ceilings were defined: 900,000 air and ground troops, with a sub-limit of 700,000 for ground troops. These ceilings would require reductions from existing levels. NATO would have to cut about 90,000 ground troops — a significant number, but insufficient to reduce seriously the financial burdens of defence for individual countries. The extent to which the Warsaw Pact would have to cut has been a matter of dispute, since both sides have worked from conflicting data: NATO data shows Warsaw Pact superiority, whereas Pact data, conveniently, shows virtual parity already. This discrepancy soon became the major obstacle to agreement and is examined in detail in Appendix 6.

Even if this problem were solved, however, to describe the resultant parity as a genuine military balance would be quite misleading. Two underlying asymmetries, barely touched by MBFR, work in favour of the Warsaw Pact. The first is the product of geography and thus not amenable to negotiation. The second derives from the armament and disposition of Soviet forces based in Eastern Europe and the tactical doctrine which supports them. These two asymmetries are important because of their critical bearing on both blocs' capacity to mobilize.

Only manpower would be subject to serious controls (although the East has always argued for the inclusion of armaments). The controls would apply within an artificial guidelines area — Benelux, the two Germanies, Poland and Czechoslovakia — so there would be no restrictions on reinforcements based in the western Soviet Union.

Objectives other than parity have tended to be thwarted. For example, the East has been anxious that West German forces should not eventually dwarf all the others. The Germans did not like being singled out for special attention, and the other members of NATO objected to inhibitions on intra-alliance adjustments of

Mutual and balanced force reductions

forces. They have therefore resisted Warsaw Pact proposals for national sub-ceilings.

An interesting feature of this argument is that other NATO members have had similar views on the need to contain any future West German military expansion. When postwar rearmament for Germany was agreed to in Paris in 1954, conditions were established then which limited its military growth to a ceiling of 12 divisions and 1,000 combat aircraft. An unpublished Protocol to the Paris Agreements of 1954 placed a manpower ceiling on the Bundeswehr (air, land and sea) of 500,000 active-duty personnel. At present the Bundeswehr contains 495,000 men, 12 divisions and about 600 combat aircraft, and is thus already effectively constrained by a manpower ceiling imposed by its allies.

For its part, NATO has been anxious to remove some of the sharpness from Soviet combat capabilities. Its original 1973 proposal required the removal of a whole tank army of 68,000 troops and 1,700 tanks. The Soviet Union was never very impressed with this idea: NATO offered little in return, and the only suitable Soviet tank army was the First Guards tank army in East Germany, whose removal would have undermined its whole capability in that area. Over time, the NATO position was drastically modified. By the end of the 1970s the number of troops required to leave was only 30,000 and, instead of requiring a whole tank army to depart, NATO was prepared to accept 1,700 tanks from a variety of units. This meant that the tanks most likely to leave would be obsolete, so no restraints would be put on the disposition of new tanks, and no reductions would be made in the sort of equipment that is essential to a tank army. The most recent proposal envisaged no equipment reductions and a troop cut of only 11,500 for the Soviet Union — a sixth of that originally proposed.

In December 1975, in order to encourage the Soviet Union to remove its tanks, NATO offered to make a concessionary withdrawal of 1,000 US nuclear warheads and 90 delivery vehicles (36 *Pershing* I missiles and 54 F-4 aircraft). The removal of delivery vehicles was the most substantial part of this offer and caused some disquiet in NATO. The Soviet Union accepted the proposals on 'nukes for tanks', but only as a one-for-one trade.

On 6 October 1979, in an effort to persuade NATO not to modernize its long-range theatre nuclear forces, President Brezhnev

Mutual and balanced force reductions

made a unilateral gesture of removing 20,000 men and 1,000 tanks from East Germany. In December 1979, NATO took the opportunity to make its own unilateral gesture, and removed 1,000 warheads but no delivery vehicles, arguing that the appropriate forum to discuss delivery vehicles was now SALT. It then dropped the 'nukes for tanks' trade in a revised MBFR proposal.

The inability to make any dent in Soviet capabilities for surprise attack, and the vexed question of data, appear to have persuaded NATO (at US urging) to turn the negotiations into something quite different, by playing down the force reductions side of the whole enterprise and emphasizing 'associated measures'. This new departure was reflected in the proposal of December 1979 and reached its logical conclusion with the December 1985 proposal of notional reductions and a stringent verification regime. The verification regime, it should be noted, was now required not so much to verify reductions as to verify a statement of the current position. It would essentially be a three-year audit. Although the Soviet Union has made some concessions on the verification question, the West's proposals would seem to be too radical to be accepted.

The data question had appeared to be a contest between truth and error, since any attempt to fudge the answer would mean giving up the principle of firm verification based on an accurate (as well as agreed) data base. Trading on the discrepancy would have undermined confidence in any eventual treaty. To avoid a compromise on data, NATO has compromised on substance. It has not so much conceded the Warsaw Pact position as watered down its own proposals to the point where no discussions worthy of mention are underway. The East has similarly watered down its proposals. The cuts now under discussion are probably equivalent to the number of troops malingering on any given day.

All this makes MBFR the most dispensable of the current negotiations. Termination has been judged unwise in recent years, for it would have been taken as part of a general attack on arms control. However, if arms control can now proceed in more productive areas, it might be sensible to wind the whole thing up. The most likely agreement would take the form of initial reductions somewhere between the Warsaw Pact and NATO proposals (11,000 to 11,500 for the Warsaw Pact and 5,000 to 6,500 for NATO), with a somewhat less stringent verification regime

Mutual and balanced force reductions

than that proposed by NATO, which would probably be insufficient to confirm the Warsaw Pact's figures one way or the other and thus provide insufficient confidence for a move to something more substantial. In April 1986, Mr Gorbachev hinted that one way out of the deadlock in Vienna would be to move discussions of arms reductions to a new forum. He suggested that the guidelines could be widened — 'from the Atlantic to the Urals' — to bring in all the countries of Europe; in other words, he seemed to be seeking to transfer all these issues to the next stage of the Conference on Disarmament in Europe, which is discussed in the next chapter, or even to an entirely new forum. The inclusion of all Europe meant that the context for the discussion of numbers would change. In June the Warsaw Pact outlined its ideas: mutual reductions of 100,000 to 150,000 troops within two years, including tactical air forces and a cut in short-range nuclear forces; 25 per cent cuts in alliance strengths in the 1990s; and intrusive verification (though not as intrusive as NATO would like). For its part, NATO set up a high-level working-group and promised 'bold' new ideas. The issue remains: can *any* regionally based force-reductions exercise be satisfactory, given the sheer complexity of the subject-matter?

The major risk is that deadlocked negotiations impose a 'planning blight' on NATO's Central Front. There are a number of pressures for change in the Alliance's conventional capabilities: the need to find resource savings, demographic changes, the desire to raise the nuclear threshold, interest in emerging technologies, proposals for greater role specialization, new tactical ideas, dissatisfaction with the disposition of NATO forces, and so on. These various pressures by no means point in a single direction. It would be unfortunate if the caution and inflexibility that can result from the actual practice of negotiating arms control, as well as from the regime that might eventually be agreed, were to constrain any possible changes and deny the Alliance the flexibility that it might need to rearrange its forces in a more sensible manner. This is not to say that the need for crisis stability will play no part in such a rearrangement. On the contrary, crisis stability might be better served a different approach from the traditional one exemplified by MBFR. Such an approach might be found in discussions on confidence-building measures.

8
CONFIDENCE-BUILDING MEASURES

Confidence-building measures (CBMs) have been seized upon in recent years as the last best hope of arms control. They are presented as addressing the real issue, fear of surprise attack, rather than the more artificial question of force levels. The focus is on the factors that actually shape each side's perceptions, and on providing evidence of a lack of menace. It is hoped that the political benefit of more relaxed relations will result directly from the military benefit of a reduced threat of surprise attack.

The stress is on the way one side presents its force posture to the other, rather than on changes in that posture. All the factors that determine one state's perception of the military threat posed by another are relevant to CBMs, especially military dispositions and activities which might have an innocent explanation but which create suspicions on the other side. Proposals in this area have increasingly taken the form of establishing known and predictable military routines, so that any departure from the norm would soon be noticed.

Accidental war

The origins of CBMs can be traced to a number of distinct areas of concern. One long-standing anxiety, ever since the 1950s, has been that war might occur by accident or miscalculation, as a result of technical malfunction, human failure, unauthorized action or a misinterpreted incident. Recognizing that speedy communication could ensure that no disastrous steps were taken in panic, the superpowers set up, in 1963, a direct communications link — the 'hot line' — for use in emergencies. In September 1971 the two superpowers signed the Agreement on Measures to Reduce the Risk of Outbreak of Nuclear War. This involved pledges to maintain and improve organizational and technical safeguards against accidental or unauthorized use of nuclear weapons; arrangements for immediate notification should a risk of war arise from such incidents, or from detection of unidentified objects on early warning systems, or from any other unexplained incidents involving a possible detonation of a nuclear weapon; and advance notification of any planned missile launches beyond the territory of the launching party and in the direction of the other party.

This approach has for the most part been confined to the very special questions of nuclear war, and has been handled by the nuclear powers. (It is quite separate from concern about deliberate military preparations.) In recent years interest has revived, and there has been new research on the various ways in which the decision-making of an anxious adversary might be distorted by a variety of organizational and technical factors such as the raising of the alert status of nuclear forces or large-scale missile tests or the risk of malfunction in command and control systems. The conclusions of this research have already been reflected in the policies of the two sides.

One of the few recent agreements has been to improve the hot line, which provides direct communication in times of crisis. In the spring of 1983, the United States made proposals for advance notice of all ballistic-missile test launches, mass bomber take-offs and the flushing out from port of large numbers of SSBNs. The Soviet Union in its counterproposals has stressed measures with a larger political content: the banning of foreign bombers and aircraft carriers from zones near each superpower; advance notice of mass take-offs of forward-based aircraft (i.e., US aircraft in Europe); and the establishment of zones in which there can be no anti-submarine operations. This last point reflects its anxiety that Western strengths in anti-submarine warfare render its own submarine-based deterrent far less secure than the US counterpart. Some interest has been shown in the notification of missile tests, though not those taking place individually on Soviet territory.

There is an obvious value in prohibiting surges of nuclear

Confidence-building measures

activity, which could make an opponent jumpy at the best of times and push him into precipitate action at the worst. Nor is there any reason in principle why such prohibitions could not be agreed. They would undermine attempts to plan for, let alone set in motion, large-scale and complex nuclear operations, inasmuch as they could not be practised in peacetime. It is unlikely that any major flexing of nuclear muscles in this way would ever seem appropriate in a crisis, but it is as well to be sure.

The Soviet approach draws attention to the movement of forces as a potential hazard. If offensive forces are pushed forward into threatening positions, an anxious adversary might get nervous about the growing vulnerability of key elements of its military power; at the same time, of course, the forces pushed forward are also likely to be making themselves more vulnerable. There has been some concern that naval activity around Northern Europe could lead to an incident. Agreements already exist to handle incidents at sea, but these could be inadequate if there were major movements underway. Here, however, we hit a major snag: measures that are essentially precautionary in nature can appear provocative. This risk, though, is accepted because of the greater risks believed to be involved in not taking precautions. More seriously, provocation — or at least a display of resolve and preparation — is sometimes intended. Crisis management may be mainly about preventing a conflict of interest leading to war; but that is rarely taken to mean abandoning vital interests.

Surprise attack

The discussion so far has moved on from the consideration of technical malfunctions to the way in which an opponent's intentions will be interpreted in a crisis. In such circumstances there is often a thin line between demonstrating a willingness to defend vital interests and appearing to prepare for aggressive action. It is important to widen that line. That can best be done by ensuring that, whatever the intentions, aggression could not be mounted effectively. Since a key advantage of the aggressor is surprise, measures to increase warning time can play an important stabilizing role.

In the 1950s, both sides made proposals to reduce the risks of surprise attack. These plans reflected the views at that time of the likely political inspiration of an attack: the East was fearful of the implications of Western insistence on the reunification of Germany; the West was concerned about the East's continued pressure on West Berlin.

Warsaw Pact proposals sought to remove the presumed Western motive by seeking the recognition of the existence of two Germanies. Other proposals were directed against US nuclear-armed aircraft based in Europe and the introduction of nuclear weapons into West Germany on a dual-key basis. Ideas to counter surprise attack involved having control posts at railway junctions, major ports and highways (twice as many in the West as in the East), and aerial surveys in the key area of vulnerability.

The West meanwhile was still unwilling to confirm the Soviet postwar occupation of Eastern Europe. Nor could it accept the exclusion of facilities in the Soviet Union, from where, it was suspected, aggression was most likely to be mounted, and inadequate arrangements for inspection of those facilities that were included. It felt that adequate surveillance would make surprise attack extremely difficult, if not impossible, and, in 1955, President Eisenhower put forward his 'Open Skies' formula, which would have allowed aerial overflights to ensure that no suspicious preparations were underway. During the decade, ideas were developed for inspection posts that would have unrestricted communications and would be able to check on areas that aerial inspection had revealed to be suspicious. The growing US concern over strategic first strikes meant that the facilities to be covered would include those for missile-launching and air bases.

The clash between these different ideas came in November 1958 at an extremely brief meeting of US and Soviet experts to discuss surprise attacks, during which the two delegations talked past each other, adjourned and never met again. The ideas remained around for a few years, but were increasingly neglected. The overall strategic balance, as well as nuclear proliferation, began to dominate arms control. The settling of the political problems of the two Germanies and Berlin by direct diplomatic means removed not only a major obstacle to some of the original Warsaw Pact concepts, but also its main interest in promoting the concepts.

In the 1970s, the West became concerned at the overt development of a Soviet conventional force structure that was suitable for swift mobilization and surprise attack and would deny NATO the time required to brace itself to respond. As a result, the earlier interest in a surveillance regime as one means of reducing the opportunities for surprise re-emerged.

Verification

A final factor encouraging a broader surveillance regime has been the need to verify traditional arms control agreements, which are seen to depend on adequate means of monitoring compliance. In the 1950s and early 1960s, this was a serious constraint in the moves towards a comprehensive test ban, for the only way to be absolutely sure that nothing untoward was going on was actually to go to scenes of potential crimes and search for clues of wrongdoing. Since the relevant sites were likely to be sensitive military facilities, such visits could be occasions for espionage. This worried the secrecy-minded Soviet Union, which opposed the principle of on-site inspection.

During the 1960s, this constraint began to be removed with the development of reconnaissance satellites, as well as other forms of electronic surveillance, which made it possible to achieve extraordinary coverage of other countries' military capabilities from secure and unobtrusive vantage points. The high-quality information obtained could be used to check on compliance with agreements, as a part of normal intelligence work.

The first SALT treaty in 1972 explicitly acknowledged the role of these 'national technical means of verification', and it was assumed that they would provide the basis for confidence in compliance in all future arms control agreements. The furtherance of arms control became linked to the improvement and refinement of the means of verification, so that more could be watched continuously and in greater detail than before.

It is not enough, however, to identify violations. Unless the offence can be detected and stopped early enough, there must be some redress. In practice, the only available sanctions are to abrogate the agreement in order to deny the other side unilateral advantage, and to allow the resultant mistrust to sour all relations. In any assessment of the sources of mistrust, suspicion of non-compliance may be as important as actual proof.

This is in fact what has happened. The United States has made regular complaints about Soviet violations of a variety of agreements. The evidence in many of these cases has suggested something less than a 'smoking gun', although, in one case, the phased-array radar at Krasnayorsk, most independent observers agree that the US allegations have substance. The Soviet Union has made counter-allegations. Whatever the merits of either side's arguments, the net effect has been to undermine support for the overall idea of arms agreements and increase rather than decrease mutual suspicions.

These alleged violations were eventually used by the Reagan administration as the reason for abandoning the SALT II treaty in June 1986. This was despite the fact that those areas of the treaty in which the Soviet Union had complied had been responsible for holding down numbers of missile launchers and warheads, and that the Soviet Union was better placed to take advantage of an end to treaty constraints. More serious than the end of an unratified treaty, which — if ratified — would have already expired the previous December, was the political message. If President Reagan believed that the Soviet Union was cheating on a treaty which candidate Reagan had described in 1980 as 'fatally flawed' in so favouring the USSR, what hope was there that an arms control agreement which met American interests could be adequately verified?

A number of the US allegations reflected ambiguities in treaty language as well as in intelligence data. This points to the danger of a badly drafted agreement, with grey areas that can be explored in the search for loopholes. Military programmes can be supported just to the boundaries of the agreement, provisions interpreted in a legal but dubious manner to avoid alarming some powerful military lobby, and so on. Such an approach to treaty obligations will offend the other side, as being against the 'spirit' of the agreement even if within the letter of the law, and will excuse similarly liberal interpretations of awkward provisions by way of response.

Thus, confidence in the other side's integrity may depend on what is going on despite negotiated agreements, or at least in ambiguous areas left by these agreements. Moreover, it is often dependent not on what goes on in secret, but on what goes on overtly. Suspicions are then likely to extend to what is not known:

activities that cannot be viewed readily, and may not need to be viewed under the provisions of a treaty, might be considered to be pregnant with danger. In these conditions, the more that is known, the more particular fears may be calmed, even if no direct questions of treaty-compliance are at stake. There is no single demarcation line between what does and does not need to be verified if the aim is to encourage confidence rather than allay suspicions of specific acts of non-compliance.

The optimism surrounding strategic arms control in the early 1970s was based on the assumption that relevant military activity could now be monitored from outside a country's border by powerful radars and satellites (known as the 'national technical means of verification'). They would be intrusive without being obtrusive. The limits to national technical means may now have been reached. Reconnaissance satellites are most suitable for monitoring quantities of weapons. As the negotiations have become concerned with the quality — number of warheads, accuracy or range — the challenges to the means of verification have grown. Weapons such as the cruise missile are more mobile and versatile, and impede attempts to keep a check on the other side's force structure. Attempting to watch movements of manpower, as in MBFR, poses its own problems because of the ease of concealment, the high turnover of personnel and the vast amount of everyday activity.

It often seems in negotiations on arms control that the issue of verification is the dominant one, and that in the most difficult areas the requirements for verification are likely to have more impact than the actual agreements being monitored. Take for example the question of chemical weapons. A 'no first use' agreement on this was signed in the 1920s, but stocks are still held 'just in case'. NATO has been concerned with apparent Soviet preparedness to use chemical weapons and the United States is starting to modernize its own arsenal. It is not altogether clear that great military advantages could be obtained by using these weapons, except that the threat to use them would force troops to wear cumbersome protective gear (but so might the threat of battlefield nuclear use). Chemical weapons excite special horror, so any agreement to ban them would be popular as well as ease one area of uncertainty in military planning. However, since any country with a serious chemicals industry can produce chemical weapons

Confidence-building measures

(as Iraq has demonstrated), the verification requirements must of necessity be extremely intrusive and even commercially sensitive. Not surprisingly, this is the main stumbling-block to an agreement.

Verification is therefore not automatic; it requires cooperation. In SALT I, in 1972, it was implied that only passive cooperation was required. There was to be no interference with the means of verification themselves — no knocking out spy satellites. It was explicitly stated that no changes were required in 'current construction, assembly, conversion or overhaul practices' to ease verification. Yet, in the 1979 SALT II treaty, mention was made of a whole series of 'cooperative measures', such as exchanges of data, not coding test data, and not concealing missiles. When the Carter administration decided to move to a mobile basing mode for its new MX ICBM, it was accepted that verifiability had to be a design feature, despite the actual purpose of using a form of deception to ensure survival in a surprise attack.

Finally, in MBFR, NATO has proposed measures which would involve air or ground inspections of suspicious activities on request, and permanent observers at the exit and entry points into the guidelines area to check on movements, as well as exchanges of data and prior notification of movements.

Transparency

Following this trend, confidence-building can be directly related to the opening up of all military activity to sustained scrutiny. The key concept is 'transparency', which involves moving from traditional levels of military secrecy towards a more open system in which less and less is left to the imagination. Much of what is proposed in the name of confidence-building is in fact a general assault on secrecy, and indeed some measures demanded for 'verification' already go beyond what is strictly required (especially when the less advertised forms of information collection are taken into account). Not surprisingly, the Soviet Union is inherently suspicious of the concept of transparency, which it considers another word for espionage, and therefore of the more ambitious Western proposals for verification. It prefers reassuring statements of political and military intent as more likely sources of confidence.

Confidence-building measures

The first CBMs were agreed at the Conference on Security and Cooperation in Europe, which produced a Final Act in Helsinki in 1975. This introduced the following modest measures: an agreement to notify all 35 participating countries, not less than 21 days in advance, of ground-force manoeuvres (with or without air and naval components) which exceeded a total of 25,000 personnel; voluntary notification of sub-threshold manoeuvres and other military movements; and the invitation of observers to manoeuvres of any size.

The implementation of this agreement was mixed. The commitments made at Helsinki were honoured in so far as there was notification of exercises above the threshold level. The Warsaw Pact showed only grudging regard for voluntary CBMs. It took until just before the first review conference of the CSCE, which began in Belgrade in October 1977, for the Soviet Union to invite observers to manoeuvres, and then this gesture was marred by the severe restrictions placed on them. In general, NATO countries have entered more into the spirit of CBMs than the Warsaw Pact, though they, too, have circumscribed the permitted observations.

In December 1980, at the start of the Madrid review conference, Western delegates complained that, since the Helsinki conference, observers had been invited to only seven out of thirteen Warsaw Pact manoeuvres above 25,000 men, whereas NATO's record was nine invitations for nine manoeuvres. NATO had also invited Pact observers to eight of its twenty manoeuvres below the 25,000 threshold, of which it had issued voluntary notifications, whereas the Warsaw Pact had notified NATO of only three small manoeuvres and invited observers to none. Even the neutral and non-aligned (NNA) countries had notified a larger number of sub-threshold manoeuvres.

This question is currently being handled at the Stockholm Conference on Confidence and Security Building Measures and Disarmament in Europe. The West has sought to improve on the 1975 position. The original CBMs applied only to a zone which extended some 25 kilometres into Soviet territory; the agreed new zone will extend to the Urals. The West's approach is to establish an agreed data base between the two sides on the current state of their force structures, and to provide a timetable at the start of each calendar year for anticipated military movements over the next twelve months. The CBMs agreed in 1975 are to be extended to cover all out-of-garrison activities over 6,000 troops and to provide 45 days' warning. Invitation to observers will be mandatory.

The East has been less enthusiastic about this approach. It has suggested only a slight reduction in the threshold level for manoeuvres. It would, however, prohibit manoeuvres above 40,000 troops (which would affect NATO far more than the Warsaw Pact). In addition, it has made attempts to limit naval manoeuvres, which again could affect NATO more. NATO is prepared to discuss only naval activity relevant to land warfare (i.e., amphibious landings).

The Warsaw Pact's emphasis has been more on declaratory measures, such as a pledge not to use nuclear weapons first. In order to achieve a compromise NATO has picked up on what it deems to be the least harmful of these — a no first use of force treaty. NATO considers this to be adequately covered by the UN Charter and has been nervous lest it serve as a basis for a push on no first use of nuclear weapons. However, in June 1984 President Reagan agreed to discuss it.

One of the most important differences between this and other negotiations is the role of the NNA countries as arbiters and sources of original ideas. Their position may indicate the form of an eventual compromise. It is as follows: there will be a reaffirmation of the principle of the non-use of force; manoeuvres of a division or more must be included in an annual calendar and notified specifically 42 days in advance; observers will be invited from all participating states; limits will be imposed on the size (no more than five divisions) and length (no more than 17 days) of the manoeuvres; there will be limits on the number of manoeuvres each year; and, in order to get round NATO's problem, once a year two manoeuvres may combine (but still not to more than seven divisions).

The details may vary, but it is now likely that future manoeuvres in Europe will be regulated in a significant manner. To what extent might this help meet the supposed objectives of CBMs? The theory and practice of CBMs suggest two quite distinct effects. Over time some measures are supposed to lead to a form of military, and possibly political, detente. If, however, relations move in exactly the opposite direction, towards a major crisis, other measures might calm the situation by preventing defensive military moves from being misinterpreted and by impeding preparations for a surprise attack. In this second sense, CBMs would operate in the same way as classic arms control, reinforcing the shared interest in avoiding war despite strong mutual antagonism. The two roles are not wholly contradictory, in that a demonstration of the implausibility of surprise attack has been considered the foundation of arms race stability and detente.

The measures discussed thus far are not sufficient to calm these fears of surprise attack. Historically, manoeuvres have been used as preparations for actual hostilities, but they are not the only way of preparing. Certainly, notification of manoeuvres does not constitute notification of risk of attack. The value of the notification procedures lies in indicating that some military routine is being followed: the more regular the pattern of activity that is established, the less easy it will be to depart from this pattern without exciting suspicions. Other measures, such as keeping large areas on each side of the likely front line as free as possible of critical pieces of equipment, indeed of whole armies, may make it impossible to achieve complete surprise.

On the other hand, once a regular pattern of activity is established, it will also be easily exploitable without alerting the victim. In addition, there may be something of a fixation with surprise that is based on the assumption that, with both sides relatively evenly balanced, the first blow will be critical. Unless we assume that the initial attack in World War III will come without any warning, we need to consider the circumstances in which fighting could begin.

These circumstances would probably involve a major political crisis in which the stakes were evidently high. In such a crisis, rather than disclaim interest in fighting, those involved would seek to demonstrate resolve and willingness to fight for their cause. They might use mobilization and manoeuvres to strengthen a diplomatic stand. In 1980, during the Polish crisis, the authorities reported fictitious manoeuvres involving Soviet and Polish troops in and around Poland in order to warn the people of their precarious position. Various measures — cancelling leave, calling up reservists and moving troops to forward positions — are features of crises (such as those in the past over Berlin) and by no means inevitably result in war, but they do tend to negate the effects of any pre-arranged CBMs.

Forcing one side unambiguously to signal hostile intent prior to actual engagement, as having to cross into a completely or partially demilitarized zone would do, does not by itself help — unless the added warning can be used to good effect. Such a zone means that border territory is not properly defended. By the time the defender has mustered his forces to move forward to meet the aggressor, the aggressor's early momentum may have carried him through the zone and into new territory. The critical issue is the speed of mobilization: that is, not just the arrival of the first wave of forces, but also the number, quality and equipment of the reserves coming up behind, including the tanks and armoured vehicles that carry them forward, and the supporting artillery and aircraft. Without the cover of a manoeuvre, the necessary large-scale preparations will provide sufficient warning to enable the prospective victim to institute countermeasures. The most important consequence of CBMs will be the limitation of the use that can be made of manoeuvres in signalling preparations for war. The agreement being negotiated at Stockholm will make it difficult to put on a *special* show of force to intimidate another country. On the other hand, if any show *is* put on, it will be a violation of the agreement, and will immediately become much more serious than would otherwise have been the case. The main value of CBMs may therefore lie in the actual process of building confidence in peacetime, and thereby helping to relax tensions so as to make it unlikely that serious crises will arise. Here again, it is necessary to be extremely cautious.

The claims made about the virtues of transparency are far more readily accepted in NATO than in the Warsaw Pact. In the East the culture of secrecy is deep-rooted. The Soviet Union sees demands for transparency as part of the West's drive to undermine its control over Eastern Europe by fostering infectious notions of freedom of movement, ideas and association, which might disturb the political equilibrium of the East. Such defensiveness does not encourage optimism that the Warsaw Pact will soon be opening up to the penetrating gaze of NATO.

Nor is there any close relationship between the transparency of each side's military posture and the amount of political tension and competition in armaments. Even without measures specifically designed to facilitate the other's observations, remarkable amounts of information can now be gleaned from satellite reconnaissance and other means of surveillance. The detail on military matters now common in the Western press, never mind in the more secret fare available to officials, indicates the quality of information available. Confirmation of what is already known may help confidence, but when information proffered in the guise of CBMs or cooperative verification is at variance with that gleaned by independent means, suspicions are likely to grow. We have already noted the problems caused by contradictory data in MBFR.

The actual operation of CBMs might also excite suspicions. Observers at Warsaw Pact manoeuvres have had restricted viewing of staged activities of slight relevance, over a short period and with the aid of low-quality binoculars. Even with better facilities, the greatest interest is always going to be in those forces that are kept hidden and in manoeuvres that remain unobserved. Without complete openness, curiosity will always be intense, and some dark and dangerous secret will be suspected. Partial openness will encourage evasive ruses and the attendant mistrust. The tension between building confidence and facilitating espionage will remain (and not only on the Eastern side).

When features of the other's force structure are revealed, the picture will not always be reassuring. A general putting on a show for his potential adversaries will not wish his troops to appear slovenly, ill-equipped and under poor command, though such a display might be extremely reassuring. A self-respecting general would want to impress with a disciplined, dedicated, fully prepared force. This may do little for the confidence of his opposite numbers, who could become convinced of the need for more strenuous exertions on their part. Greater confidence may emerge from more private observations of the other side's limitations.

Thus, the 1980 Soviet manoeuvres during the Polish crisis revealed low morale and inefficiency, yet these manoeuvres could only avoid being deemed a violation of the CSCE agreements by making favourable assumptions about the proportion of the 100,000 troops said to be taking part which was located outside the CSCE zone.

There is not necessarily a close fit between the confidence a country may have in its security position and the 'confidence' produced through formal agreements on transparency. Another example of this is the US response to recent Soviet pressure for a comprehensive test ban. If this idea had been implemented when it was first proposed in the 1950s, it would have prevented many important developments in nuclear systems. Now the relevant technology is sufficiently mature for weapon design to be only marginally affected by a complete ban. (A partial ban forced testing underground in 1963. Other agreements reached in the 1970s banned 'peaceful' nuclear explosions and detonations above 150 kilotons; they have yet to be ratified by the United States, but they are still being observed).

Because of the long history of this issue, it has taken on a symbolic importance, especially in the context of the nuclear Non-Proliferation Treaty. If a comprehensive ban were to be agreed, it would encourage confidence among non-nuclear-weapon states that the superpowers were fulfilling their obligations under Article VI of the treaty. The United States has argued that it would only sign a test ban if it were confident that the Soviet Union could not test in a clandestine manner. When Mr Gorbachev made concessions in the area of verification, the Americans made it clear that they wished to keep testing to ensure confidence in the reliability of the existing arsenal. There is thus no single source of confidence in security matters, and there can be differing views over which source is the most important. What matters most to a particular government will depend on its own sense of what most threatens its security.

Knowledge of the other side's forces makes sense only within some broader framework which will provide guidance on how to interpret data. East and West tend to view each other not only in a particular and largely unfavourable manner, but from the perspective of their own strategic theories and military doctrine. One remedy lies in regular meetings between civilians and military officials and experts from both sides. Formal CBMs therefore need to be accompanied by new institutions that would be set up to agree interpretations of measures in ambiguous situations, investigate charges of non-compliance, seek explanations of apparent transgressions, and identify possible amendments of existing CBMs and proposals for new ones. The model for this sort of activity is the Standing Consultative Commission, which has successfully dealt with problems in the implementation of the SALT accords. It is not enough for both sides just to look at each other; they must talk as well.

Confidence-building measures

There have been a number of proposals recently for crisis management centres or nuclear risk control centres, perhaps with one each in Moscow and Washington, to maintain constant contact on all relevant issues and to exchange data and insights. This idea for a superpower forum could be extended to something East-West generally or indeed to all the signatories of the CSCE. However, one suspects that the quality of the data exchange, difficult enough to attain between the superpowers, would be diluted as the number of recipients increased.

It is probably unwise anyway to expect too much from such fora. At times of real crisis, the key actors will be in the national capitals. Indeed, although it would be useful to have an institutionalized forum for ensuring that delicate East-West issues were handled discreetly at an early stage, the critical attitudes will always be those held at the highest level. This sort of forum could be no substitute for more regular contact between senior policy-makers across the East-West divide.

Declaratory measures

Lastly, what about the declaratory measures favoured by the Soviet Union? The extent to which governments wish to be seen to be acting within international law should not be underestimated. Nor, despite the suspicions of the West, should the seriousness of some Soviet proposals. There is evidence, for example, that Brezhnev's 1982 offer on no first use of nuclear weapons was the subject of considerable debate in Moscow.

However, agreements that might be difficult to sustain in practice are not necessarily so helpful. Consider, for example, the question of no first use, a proposal which has influential support within NATO countries. It is awkward to maintain the right to use nuclear weapons first. When one set of critics is reassured that first nuclear use does not mean first strike — in that it would be on a limited scale, would involve no attempt to inflict a decisive military victory, but would merely warn the aggressor of the consequences of a failure to withdraw — it then becomes necessary to explain to another set of critics why ever NATO would contemplate such a dangerous move if it could not be relied upon to turn the military tide in its favour. Attempts to counter Soviet propaganda by

Confidence-building measures

arguing that declarations of no first use are virtually worthless, especially when made by Moscow, encourage cynicism as to the value of all rules of conduct that might govern relations between states.

Should the decision to use nuclear weapons ever have to be faced, the position is likely to be different from that anticipated at a time of relative peace. NATO puts great stress on the threat of first use, yet there are many indications that the fire-break between conventional and nuclear warfare is firmly entrenched in the minds of Alliance leaders, who are unwilling to accept the logic of the first-use threat. On the other hand, a commitment to no first use might also be misleading. The fire-break is only firmly established in strategic and political theory. There can be no guarantee that it would survive in war, whatever the solemn promises made in peacetime; the actual process of escalation may well be substantially different from that anticipated prior to hostilities. More to the point, it would be surprising if any nation did assume that a war among the major powers could avoid 'going nuclear', and it would be utterly irresponsible for them to assume otherwise. That is, many of those who now urge a declaration of no first use would be horrified if, at a time of crisis, leaders of another side were suggesting that there was no need to worry about nuclear war because of the promises that had been made in happier times!

9
CONCLUSION

Much of the public debate on arms control takes as its starting-point the need to reduce the international level of armaments. At issue is how this is to be achieved. The debate can easily turn into a contest between the grand gestures of the unilateralists, who hope to send the arms race into reverse by a dramatic renunciation of a particular capability, and the caution of the multilateralists, who put their faith in painstaking diplomatic effort.

This paper has concentrated on multilateral (or more normally bilateral) efforts. The advantage of multilateralism is that it is not dependent upon the good faith of others. Both sides move in the same direction at the same pace. Negotiation should ensure that both fully understand each other's rights and obligations. Agreements that are long-term and binding, and capable of proper verification, should be able to survive all manner of political upheaval. The difficulty with unilateralism is that it is all too easy for a particular move to be reversed when international conditions change, and there is always a risk of a well-meaning gesture being taken as an opportunity rather than as an example by an adversary.

Binding agreements are preferable to protestations of good will, simply because they are likely to be much more durable. However, as this paper has sought to demonstrate, it is as well to acknowledge the complications that are introduced into the practice of multilateral or bilateral arms control as a result of the need to negotiate agreements, instead of relying on tacit understandings or reciprocated arrangements. Negotiations create their

Conclusion

own hopes and expectations. They raise the profile of particular weapons, and shape political agendas and ways of thinking about military relationships. The need to reach agreements that can withstand domestic scrutiny and be readily monitored limits the sorts of measure that can be envisaged. For all these reasons the negotiated approach is essentially managerial. Reform is much more likely to result from major changes in the political and strategic environment, or from shifts in military thinking and priorities.

Arms conrol, as it has been practised over the past couple of decades, appears to have worked best as a means of consolidating the more satisfactory aspects of the political and military status quo. It does not create favourable trends, but it can reinforce them and give them some permanence. It can also, however, reinforce adverse trends, and therefore it is unwise to push things too hard at a time when political relations are deteriorating. The effort is likely to advertise and accentuate the deterioration, rather than make things better.

Arms control is not an independent force acting upon a resistant international political and military order; it is very much shaped by that order. In addition, it has many purposes other than the ones which are normally claimed for it. It is used to reinforce the political status quo and deflect opposition, to score propaganda points and reaffirm existing doctrines, and to protect and even make a case for favoured weapon systems, as well as to reduce force levels, introduce elements of crisis stability and ease international tension.

Thus, one of the reasons why the process produces so little, and why unilateralism might be expected to suffer from similar disappointments, is that the conventional understanding of the objective is based on an oversimplified analysis. If one side's forces were no more than a response to the other, it should be possible to arrange a virtuous cycle of an arms race in reverse. Unfortunately, there are many factors shaping force structure, of which the adversary is but one. Others are the lead-time needed for the introduction of new weapons, which limits the speed of response to new developments; bureaucratic, political and industrial pressures; cultural factors; tactical doctrines; and domestic and alliance politics. Unless these factors are acknowledged, there is a risk of frustration and disappointment.

Conclusion

Hence the importance of clarity with regard to objectives. The broad aims of crisis stability and arms race stability mean little unless the sources of actual and potential instability have been realistically identified. As argued earlier, in neither case is the position clear-cut. A good measure of crisis stability already seems to exist, in that there is every incentive to avoid initiating an East-West war. The concept of arms race stability has never been sufficiently developed to take account of the multitude of factors that influence the shape and content of armed forces. Via the notions of parity and, to a lesser extent, sufficiency the concept has been turned into something suitable for negotiating purposes, but at the cost of much strategic relevance and without the pay-off in the negotiations for which many hoped.

All these ideas have been developed largely with nuclear arms control in mind. Although success has proved elusive, it is still possible to imagine eventual deals that would bring the negotiations to a satisfactory conclusion. As already noted, though, it is precisely because the strategic relationship is not especially unstable in the nuclear area that agreement is possible. In particular, force levels in this category can be manipulated to make what are in effect large political statements.

However, the more the nuclear area is brought under some control — either through agreements or the natural course of events — the more important the conventional area becomes. The sad story of MBFR highlights the difficulty of applying the same concepts to conventional forces. It may even be futile to expect to be able to design an arms regime for Europe in which every weapon will have its assigned place and all forces will be kept in a strict ratio to those of potential adversaries. Meanwhile, the progress with confidence-building measures is more encouraging, since these relate to issues of crisis stability. Because wars tend to start from the bottom up, as it were, rather than from the top down, there is a powerful argument for looking closely at the mechanisms by which tension might turn into war through misjudged measures of crisis management, such as precipitate mobilization, the raising of alert status or movements out of garrison.

The most valuable result of arms control negotiations in the conventional area, and to some extent in the nuclear, might be a greater degree of predictability and a sense of the routines of both

Conclusion

sides. The value of this should not be underestimated. It undermines various forms of 'worst-case analysis', by which it is suggested that future forces should be planned to anticipate the worst that the other side can do, and it produces important barriers against departures from the norm. It does, though, create the risk that the importance of *any* new departure, however innocent, will be heightened.

If arms control is to be an instrument of more radical changes, two conditions are necessary: improved political relations, and complementary trends in strategic thinking. Thus, for example, the possibilities for deep cuts in strategic nuclear arsenals and the elimination of intermediate nuclear forces have arisen because of a decline in the role that nuclear weapons are seen to be playing in security policies. That decline has not gone far enough for moves beyond those currently proposed.

Arms control can therefore mark important changes, but by and large it serves to consolidate and reaffirm the status quo against change. Even those more radically inclined tend to argue for a freeze — in the development, testing, production and deployment of new nuclear weapons — as if any change is likely to make things worse. The idea is unremarkable in itself, except that it freezes the more unstable parts of the inventory along with the stable and, being so comprehensive in scope, promises something of a nightmare negotiation.

At the moment the alternative to arms control in Europe is not an arms race; it may actually be a decline in weapons. There is pressure on resources and therefore an interest in using what is available more efficiently. There is also an interesting debate underway on conventional strategy as a whole. A number of important issues have been raised: the maldeployment of forces in Germany; communications links and the interoperability of equipment; the advisability of opting for small numbers of sophisticated weapons rather than larger numbers of more basic ones, and of trading mobility for firepower; and improving front-line strengths as against the speed of reinforcement from across the Atlantic or the number and quality of local reserves.

We have noted the danger that arms control can distort military planning, not so much by foreclosing attractive options, but by creating unnecessary requirements. The notion of parity is so embedded in the whole culture of arms control that it has come to

Conclusion

be seen as a worthwhile strategic end in itself. Yet at a time of tight budgets and difficult choices, matching forces in order to achieve some notional equilibrium is the least useful approach, particularly in the conventional area. NATO's security problem is different from that of the Warsaw Pact; its forces should be organized as effectively as possible for a strong defence where it matters, even if this involves conceding numerical superiority in some areas. The risk lies in confusing stability with the status quo.

There is a danger in congealing the current force structure. We may want fewer tanks and more light combat aircraft, but a systematic setting of numbers and standards for all types of forces would leave little flexibility. A ceiling soon becomes a norm which then has to be met if only to avoid a unilateral concession. Yet, if we choose to deal with battlefield nuclear weapons, the best approach may be to remove the weapons altogether. In this area, a lack of negotiations has not precluded a considered strategic judgment to cut stockpiles. The level of NATO's nuclear stockpile has been reduced in the 1980s, and there is still pressure — and room — for further cuts. It is doubtful that this could have happened if battlefield systems had been the subject of negotiations.

A similar point might be made in the political area. Arms control has never been anything other than a subsidiary motor for detente, and it was rarely a reliable indication of its state of health. At its most modest, detente was about the settlement of the postwar boundaries of Europe, and, at its most ambitious, it was about working out a general understanding on the relations among the major powers, including their conduct in the Third World. The problems with establishing detente in either form have been political more than military. It is arguable that the greatest damage to detente in the West in the later 1970s came as a result of Soviet adventures in the Third World, while the damage in the East resulted from fears that internal political problems were being exacerbated by Western interference. A revival of detente, as opposed to the current modest easing of relations, would certainly require that the issues of 'non-interference in political affairs' and 'codes of conduct in the Third World' be dealt with.

Europe itself remains quite stable, and attempts to design arms control to undermine alliances or spheres of influence have been thwarted. It may be that Europe already enjoys sufficient political and military stability, so that attempts to reinforce this stability

Conclusion

risk the loss of the flexibility that might be needed to respond either to future political change or to internal pressures for military reform. The military complexion of Europe has developed as a response to an evolving political environment, not to an arms race, and what will be needed above all else, should the political situation move into new and uncharted areas, is that any changes in the military sphere ease the process of peaceful change rather than bring about a period of high tension and danger.

What is beyond doubt is that if there is to be any progress in the future — whether it be in the form of marginal adjustments to force structure or of fundamental political changes — it cannot be made without regular and sustained communication at all levels between East and West. Indeed, it cannot be stressed too often that the basic objective of arms control — avoiding general war — is a problem of foreign policy as a whole. The need to be sensitive to the interests and concerns of the other side, and to explore the possibilities of building upon areas of mutual interest, is not just a prescription for arms control but for all contacts with the Soviet Union. That is why arms control is only likely to make progress to the extent that East-West relations are improving generally.

APPENDICES

1 Negotiating history of SALT

The first round of the Strategic Arms Limitation Talks (SALT) opened in November 1969 and was concluded successfully at the Nixon/Brezhnev summit of May 1972. There were two aspects to the agreement. First, and most important, a treaty of indefinite duration was signed limiting anti-ballistic missiles (ABMs) to 200 launchers apiece (two years later the limit was reduced to 100). This treaty remains intact, although President Reagan has recently challenged the assumptions on which it is based.

The second part of the 1972 accord was an interim agreement on offensive arms. This expired in 1977, although it is still being tacitly observed by both sides. The agreement was essentially a freeze on existing ICBM and SLBM launchers, or on those being prepared for deployment. In numerical terms this meant a significant Soviet lead, which was nevertheless believed to be balanced by the USA's qualitative advantages and its greater number of bombers. The package was ratified, but a proviso was attached by the Senate saying that future agreements must be based on strict equality (the Jackson Amendment). This requirement has haunted the negotiations ever since.

At first, progress was relatively swift in the effort to turn the interim agreement into a longer-term treaty. At a meeting in Vladivostok in November 1974, Presidents Ford and Brezhnev agreed on a framework for SALT II. This framework allowed for 2,400 ICBMs, SLBMs and bombers on each side, of which no more than 1,320 were to be missiles with multiple independently targetable re-entry vehicles (MIRVs). Unfortunately, the details turned out to be remarkably intractable. There were technical difficulties about verification as well as more fundamental

Appendices

questions over the inclusion of the US cruise missile programme and the Soviet *Backfire* bomber.

Formulae had been found to deal with these issues by the end of the Ford administration. However, the incoming Carter administration wished to put its own stamp on SALT and offered a new comprehensive proposal which ignored the common understandings embodied in the Vladivostok package. After an uncompromising Soviet rejection the administration backtracked and, by September 1977, a new compromise framework had been worked out. It took almost two years — until June 1979 — for this framework to be turned into a treaty available for signing.

The SALT II treaty was signed by the United States and the Soviet Union on 18 June 1979. SALT II consisted of: (1) a treaty which would, if ratified, have limited both sides to an equal ceiling of 2,400 ICBM and SLBM launchers and heavy bombers. By the end of 1981, the 2,400 limit would have been lowered to 2,250 for both sides. There would have been a 1,320 limit on launchers for MIRVed ICBMs, SLBMs and heavy bombers equipped with long-range ALCMs; 1,200 on launchers for MIRVed ICBMs and SLBMs; and 820 on launchers for MIRVed ICBMs. Also, the number of launchers for Soviet heavy (SS-9 and SS-18-type) ICBMs would have been limited to those already existing (308); the maximum number of warheads on current missile types was to be limited to the number already tested and to 10 on the one new type of ICBM permitted and to 14 on new SLBMs; the launch-weight and throw-weight of strategic ballistic missiles was to be held down essentially by freezing the capabilities of existing missiles and limiting the capabilities of the one new type of ICBM permitted to that of the heaviest existing 'light' ICBM, the SS-19; the number of long-range ALCMs on existing heavy bombers would have been limited to 20, and the average load for existing and future bombers to 28; (2) a Protocol placing a temporary ban on mobile ICBMs and cruise missiles to 1981; (3) 98 Agreed Statements and Common Understandings interpreting and clarifying the Treaty and Protocol; (4) a Joint Statement of Principles outlining guidelines for SALT III negotiations; and (5) a separate commitment, made by General-Secretary Brezhnev, to limit the capabilities of the Soviet *Backfire* bomber and its production to 30 per year.

Verification would be by national technical means, facilitated by a ban on deliberate concealment measures and on encryption of relevant telemetry, an agreed data base and various counting rules.

The treaty would have expired at the end of 1985. Although the United States has alleged that the USSR has not complied with key provisions of the SALT accords, President Reagan decided in the summer of 1985 that the United States would continue to comply for the time being.

A year later the President changed his mind. In June 1986, he announced that the United States would no longer be bound by the terms of the treaty. By decommissioning two *Poseidon* submarines (for reasons,

Appendices

he suggested, unconnected with the treaty), the USA would remain in 'technical' compliance. This state of affairs would last until the end of the year, when the arrival of the 131st B-52 bomber armed with cruise missiles would breach the 1,320 sub-limit. The decision might be reviewed if the Soviet Union took action to cease its alleged violations.

2 Negotiating history of START

1982

The Strategic Arms Reductions Talks (START) opened in June 1982 with a US proposal to reduce missile warheads to 5,000 for each side (from current levels of about 7,000), with a distinct ceiling of 850 for ICBM and SLBM launchers (which would require a cut of two-thirds for the Soviet Union and about one-half for the United States). A further limitation provided for only half (2,500) of the warheads being placed on land-based missiles. In a second phase the two sides would move to equal levels of throw-weight. This would have cut Soviet numbers more than the American, shifting the emphasis onto sea-based systems, with which the Soviet Union feels less comfortable. Little was offered in areas of US advantage, such as bombers and air- and sea-launched cruise missiles, except a willingness to discuss them. The proposal also tolerated large numbers of warheads on individual missiles.

The Soviet response was to set a ceiling of 1,800 ballistic missiles and bombers to be reached by 1990 (equivalent to a 25 per cent cutback), with a freedom-to-mix on numbers for each country. The United States would have to restrict overall cruise missile deployment and abandon the INF programme for Europe.

1983

In April 1983 there were signs of movement in the American position. Provisions were included for restrictions on sea- and air-launched cruise missiles. A more substantial shift followed the adoption of a Presidential Commission's advice to move away from dependence on a limited number of multiple-warhead ICBMs (such as MX) to larger numbers of small single-warhead ICBMs (known as *Midgetman*). The original US proposal would have encouraged the former approach, so there was now pressure to remove the launcher limit and just control warheads. On 9 June President Reagan offered to raise the launcher ceiling. No specific figure was mentioned formally, though something in the region of 1,200 was mentioned informally. More flexibility was demonstrated on throw-

Appendices

weight. Bombers would be limited to 400, with no more than 20 ALCMs on each. The United States would not deploy more than 3,500 ALCMs. The *Backfire* bomber (which the Soviet Union insists has no strategic role) would be counted.

A Soviet concession in July 1983 offered a sub-limit on MIRVed missiles. This was part of a general refinement of the Soviet position. A detailed schedule for the reductions was provided. 'Nuclear charges' — a Soviet term for missile warheads and nuclear weapons on bombers — were to be equalized at numbers below the current American level. At least 120 bombers could carry cruise missiles. The main stumbling-blocks remained the Soviet refusal to countenance large-scale cuts in their heavy ICBMs and the American reluctance, no longer so definite, to contemplate concessions in areas of comparative advantage, such as bombers and cruise missiles.

In October 1983, as a result of negotiations with Congress more than with the Russians, the United States offered to follow the 'build-down' principle in negotiations. According to this principle, for every new nuclear warhead introduced more than one old warhead must be removed. This penalizes launchers carrying large numbers of warheads, such as the new US missiles *Trident* II and MX, which have 9 and 10 warheads respectively and potentially more. It also shifts attention to delivery vehicles capable of carrying large loads in the existing arsenal, such as heavy bombers, which have tended to get neglected in recent US proposals. Thus build-down did not fit the established pattern of self-serving arms control proposals. At the time the USSR was suspicious of any new US idea, and the incredible complexity with which the Americans managed to convey this relatively simple concept (they offered to set up a special committee to explain it to the Soviet Union) also helped to dampen interest.

The build-down idea, when presented to the USSR, placed the greater emphasis on ICBM warheads: two old ICBM warheads would have to be destroyed for every new one, while with SLBMs the exchange was two for three. To ensure steady reductions, a minimum of five per cent annual decrease in the number of warheads deployed was also required.

1984

As a result of the argument over the entry of cruise and *Pershing* missiles into Europe at the end of 1983, no date was agreed by the Soviet START team for the resumption of talks in 1984. There were no negotiations that year.

Appendices

1985

On 7–8 January 1985 US Secretary of State George Schultz and Soviet Foreign Minister Andrei Gromyko agreed to a resumption of talks. Discussions on strategic offensive arms were one part of an 'umbrella' negotiation; intermediate-range forces and space weapons were the other two parts. This framework recognized the interrelationship between the parts while avoiding the complexities of integration.

The new talks opened in March 1985. The US proposal was not much different from the position held in previous negotiations: a limit of 5,000 warheads and 850 launchers, with the possibility of a larger number of launchers. In addition, US heavy bombers would be reduced to 400. Soviet commentators noted that this proposal omitted limitations on air-launched cruise missiles.

Soviet proposals in the spring of 1985 were for a freeze on existing missiles and no new deployments (which the Reagan administration insisted would merely confirm Soviet superiority). There was also a reiteration of proposals for 25 per cent cuts with hints of something more, dependent on the United States abandoning its Strategic Defence Initiative.

In the run-up to the November 1985 summit between President Reagan and General-Secretary Gorbachev, the USSR made a substantial new proposal. The central feature was a cut of 50 per cent in all strategic nuclear delivery vehicles and warheads. However, strategic weapons were defined (traditionally for the USSR) in terms of systems that could hit the other's territory. They included US cruise missiles and *Pershings* and other forward-based systems, but not Soviet systems of comparable range — for they could not hit the USA. On Soviet figures these cuts would therefore leave about 1,200 US launchers and some 6,500 warheads, as compared with similar numbers of Soviet launchers and about 5,000 warheads. No new weapons would be permitted. Any one leg of the triad of ICBMs, SLBMs and bombers would be limited to 60 per cent of the total number of warheads. This move would reduce the predominance of ICBM warheads in the Soviet arsenal (and also of SSBNs in the US arsenal). It would exclude the new D-5 *Trident* SLBM but not necessarily the MX ICBM. All cruise missiles with a range of over 600 kilometres would be banned.

The USA welcomed the 50 per cent reductions, but stated that the inclusion of its European-based systems was unacceptable. It was also not convinced that enough had been done to reduce the threat posed by the huge Soviet ICBM force. It therefore responded by proposing new lower ceilings of its own: a common warhead ceiling of 4,500 (about 50 per cent below current levels) and a reduction of missiles to 1,250–1,450 (40 to 50 per cent reductions on the highest Soviet levels). Throw-weight would be reduced by 50 per cent — but not to a common ceiling — from

Appendices

11,900,000 lbs for the USSR and 4,400,000 for the United States. Bombers and cruise missiles would be treated separately. The Americans were now prepared to limit their bomber force to 350 (the previous offer had been 400) and for the first time were willing to adopt a limit on air-launched cruise missiles of 1,500. There would be a ban on new 'heavy' missiles (which only the USSR has) and also on mobile missiles. This latter proposal was considered by some surprising given the emphasis that had been placed on the development of the mobile *Midgetman* ICBM. The reason given was 'inherent verification difficulties'. At the Geneva summit the 50 per cent figure for reductions was accepted, although the question '50 per cent of what?' was left unanswered.

1986

In June 1986, there were reports of a Soviet offer in which the USSR was easing its stance on SDI by allowing 'laboratory' research in return for an agreement to extend the withdrawal period from the ABM treaty from six months to 15/20 years. The USA indicated a willingness to consider an extension to five years, but still rejected any strong restrictions on research. On offensive arms, the USSR now suggested a 30 per cent cut rather than 50 per cent, but without US forward-based systems (which were to be frozen). No more than 60 per cent of the new level of 8,000 warheads could be ICBMs or SLBMs. SLCMs would be permitted on submarines, but not on surface ships.

3 Negotiating history of INF

1979

In December 1979 NATO decided to modernize its long-range theatre nuclear forces (now known as INF) with 464 *Tomahawk* cruise missiles and 108 *Pershing* ballistic missiles. In addition to this 'modernization' track there was a second 'arms control' track, which proposed negotiations with the USSR.

It was at that time assumed that these negotiations would take place within the SALT framework, and it was proposed that only American missiles from the NATO side (and not those of Britain and France) should be discussed. The restriction of future negotiations to land-based missiles reflected the popular perception of the issue at hand. Matters would also be kept simple by excluding aircraft. The culture of arms control and popular perceptions of the issues stressed the importance of missile parity, so the agreements had to be 'consistent with the principle of equality'. But

Appendices

only of *de jure* equality, for *de facto* equality would confirm the idea of a European strategic balance, separate from the superpower balance. In terms of NATO doctrine, this would mean 'decoupling'. For NATO, the problem lay in combining two contradictory objectives.

The first Soviet offer designed to head off the introduction of these new missiles came in a speech by President Brezhnev on 6 October 1979. He said that the Soviet Union was ready 'to reduce, compared with the present level, the quantity of medium-range nuclear missiles deployed in the western parts of the Soviet Union: but, of course, only in the event that there is no additional deployment of medium-range missiles in Western Europe.' In the period leading up to 12 December, this offer was stressed, although its ambiguities were never clarified, particularly as to whether SS-20 numbers were to be reduced.

1980

After the NATO decision, the main question was whether the Soviet Union would agree to talk at all. Its initial reaction was that the basis for talks had been destroyed by both the NATO decision and the US failure to ratify SALT II. However, by July and Chancellor Schmidt's visit to Moscow, a new basis had been found.

It was now agreed to discuss issues 'relating to medium-range weapons' (but not to implement any accords) prior to ratification of SALT II. However, the discussions would need to involve US forward-based nuclear weapons, namely, the US systems based in Europe that were capable of hitting Soviet territory. The other long-standing Soviet objective, the inclusion of British and French forces, appeared to have been postponed. From October to November 1980, preliminary discussions between America and Soviet teams on theatre nuclear arms control took place in Geneva.

1981

Discussions were then held up as a result of the US presidential elections. The talks reopened in November 1981. The initial US position was the 'zero option', according to which the United States would forgo its modernization if the Soviet Union abandoned all its SS-4s, SS-5s, and SS-20s. In terms of concentrating on land-based missiles and looking for global rather than regional application, the US position was in line with that adopted in December 1979. However, the readiness to contemplate no intermediate nuclear forces was at variance with received NATO doctrine, which stressed the need for some such forces to couple the US nuclear arsenal with the defence of Europe, irrespective of the level of comparable systems on the Eastern side. The Americans decided against including a ban on the shorter-range SS-22 missile, also capable of hitting

Appendices

deep into Western Europe, since this would have made its position even less negotiable than it already was.

1982

The Soviet position was laid down in a draft treaty of May 1982. This envisaged the two sides going down to 300 delivery systems within five years of the treaty coming into force. The implications of this proposal could only be worked out with reference to the Soviet presentation of the European nuclear balance (see Appendix 4). On the Soviet count, the result of the implementation of its proposals would have been the expulsion from the European continent of all American nuclear aircraft which could possibly strike the Soviet Union (those which might strike its Warsaw Pact allies do not seem to cause quite so much upset), while the Soviet Union was required mainly to relinquish its older missiles and aircraft. This negotiating position was carefully framed so that even an agreement among the allies to substitute US systems for those of France and Britain was ruled out, as was the introduction of any new type of weapon.

In this way the European forces appeared as fixtures using up all of the NATO account. The objective was clearly to get at the American, not the European, forces. The 300 ceiling was made up to 162 missiles and 138 aircraft. All the missiles were to be British and French and so, according to the Soviet figures, were all but 45 of the aircraft. And, as the 65 FB-111s based in the United States were also counted, the Americans were left with an allowance of minus twenty aircraft in Europe, a position that was as non-negotiable as, and far more contrived than, the zero option.

In December 1982, Mr Andropov modified the formula to allow for a specific deal, relating the number of SS-20s to British and French missiles (162). This change underlined the Soviet preoccupation with getting the Americans out of Europe rather than with cutting the European forces. However, the proposal did put the British and French forces at centre stage. For the first time a specific limit on numbers of SS-20s was offered, but there was no move away from the previous position, which included aircraft. Aircraft would still have to be reduced.

1983

In a later amendment, of May 1983, Andropov agreed to count warheads rather than launchers, but when note is taken of Moscow's assumptions on the number of warheads on current British and French missiles (which as it happens are exaggerated in the case of the UK), the net result was the same as the previous offer, with the Soviet Union still allowed some 160 SS-20s.

A concession of autumn 1983 brought the numbers down to 140 SS-20s

Appendices

and suggested that weapons removed from Europe would not simply be transferred to Asia. Right at the end of the 1983 negotiations, the Russians hinted that they might even go down to around 120 SS-20s, and not tie these numbers closely to the British and French forces, but they then publicly denied any such concession.

During 1983 the US position was also gradually modified. Although it did not renounce the zero option, the United States proposed in March an interim offer, based on the same principles as before, except that now it accepted that both sides would have some missiles (the optimum number probably being at about 300 warheads each). In October the American position moved further. There was still an insistence on equality in global allowances, but the Americans promised not to match the Soviet Union in its Asian numbers, and hinted that there could be concessions on *Pershing*. In November they put forward a global figure of 420 warheads. Assuming a 2:1 ratio between the Soviet European and Asian deployments, this would leave about 95 SS-20s (with three warheads each) in Europe.

For the USSR, all the US proposals meant giving up something in place in return for something only in plans, and leaving a Western advantage in strike aircraft untouched, along with the British and French missiles. Under the interim offer they would even have had to tolerate the new NATO missiles. The arrival of the first *Pershings* was deemed so intolerable that, in November 1983, the Soviet Union walked out of the talks.

The only attempt to work out a possible compromise came in the summer of 1982, when the two chief negotiators drafted their informal version of an eventual agreement which most observers consider to have represented the best deal available: a US compromise of no *Pershings* and no global ceilings in return for a Soviet acceptance of some cruise and no close tie to the British and French forces. The USSR would have retained 75 SS-20s facing Europe, and the USA 75 GLCM launchers (300 actual missiles). Each side would have reduced its nuclear-capable aircraft to 150, and the USSR would have frozen its SS-20s in the Far East. This deal was rejected by both governments. It is easier to see why the Soviet side rejected it than why the United States did, since the Soviets were required under this deal (known as the 'walk in the woods') to make the major concessions of principle. The Soviet interest appeared to be in the link with a summit between the US and Soviet leaders, and this interest was lost when the Americans made it clear they did not believe that the time was ripe for such a meeting. The US rejection of the deal was based on a desire to hold on to some of the more capable *Pershing* missiles.

1985

Talks did not resume until March 1985, as one part of the new umbrella negotiations. The Soviet leadership no longer made the removal of the NATO missiles already deployed a precondition, although it did indicate that a freeze on further deployments would be helpful. The US opening position was based on that of November 1983: the 'ultimate goal' was the 'complete elimination' of this entire class of missiles, but the USA was ready to consider 'interim' steps, such as a balance at 'equal levels of warheads in a global context'. To sweeten the pill, the United States would not necessarily deploy its total allowance in Europe. Nor would the full complement of 108 *Pershings* necessarily be deployed. There was also a willingness to talk about aircraft limitations.

The Soviet position was that existing arsenals should be frozen and new deployments terminated. On 7 April General-Secretary Gorbachev announced a moratorium on the deployment of SS-20s until November. The Americans observed that a freeze would suit the Soviet Union, since at the time it enjoyed an advantage of eight to one.

On October 3, in Paris, Gorbachev unveiled a new position. The key points were that progress on strategic arms and space weapons would not now be dependent on agreement on European systems; and the proposal of direct talks with Britain and France (which Britain and France immediately rejected). But the most striking difference was that the US systems that had been included in previous Soviet INF positions were now also included in the total for US strategic forces, which were to be subject to a 50 per cent cut. The Soviet position was by no means internally consistent, in that it could be interpreted as easing the eventual merger of INF and START, but then keeping the two quite separate. At one point all cruise missiles were to be banned; elsewhere provision was made for the air-launched variant.

The US counter-proposal, made on 13 November, just before the Geneva summit, involved a curb on the *Pershing* and cruise missiles in place at the end of 1985 (140) in return for a Soviet agreement to reduce SS-20 launchers within range of NATO Europe to the same number. This suggestion accepted the Soviet figure for the United States under its freeze proposal, but denied the Soviet Union further SS-20s as compensation for the UK and French forces. There would be a freedom-to-mix between systems, but one approach would be to have roughly equivalent warheads: for example, 420 (3×140) SS-20 warheads matched by 396 (4×99) cruise and 41 *Pershing*. The USA would not be required to abandon *Pershing*, but the logic of the proposal would be to discourage more than 45. The Soviet Union would also be required to reduce SS-20s in Asia by the same proportion, and there would be appropriate constraints on shorter-range systems. The agreed statement following the Reagan/Gorbachev summit referred to the 'idea of an interim INF agreement'.

1986

On 15 January 1986, Mr Gorbachev put forward a zero option of his own, in the context of his more ambitious project for the total elimination of nuclear weapons by the end of the century. The first stage of this project, to be completed within five to eight years, was to

> ... include the adoption and implementation of the decision on the complete elimination of intermediate-range missiles of the USSR and the USA in the European zone, both ballistic and cruise missiles, as a first step towards ridding the European continent of nuclear weapons.
> At the same time the United States should undertake not to transfer its strategic and medium-range missiles to other countries, while Britain and France should pledge not to build up their respective nuclear arsenals.

This was a startling shift in the Soviet position and suggested that the buildup on the NATO side had caused a major reappraisal in Moscow. Soviet sources indicated that a deal of this sort did not depend on progress on SDI, and that as a matter of course, should *Pershing* be removed, the short-range systems placed in East Germany and Czechoslovakia in 1984 would also be taken away. Furthermore, there were assurances that systems would actually be destroyed rather than merely placed somewhere else.

The Reagan administration was pleased to see its own idea — of the zero option — at the centre of a Soviet proposal. There were, however, two large problems with the Gorbachev version. First, although the Soviet proposal did not preclude modernization of British and French forces but only a buildup, in practice the modernization programmes currently in train would be severely curtailed. Neither the British nor the French government would find this acceptable. Second, no constraints were proposed on Soviet SS-20s based east of the Urals.

The initial US instinct was to accept the Soviet proposal, but refuse limits on Britain and France and insist on a 50 per cent cut in Soviet Far Eastern forces. However, the Japanese were unhappy with this, insisting that Asia should not be treated differently from Europe. On 24 February the United States tabled its response. It called for speedier and more drastic action in the elimination of *all* intermediate nuclear forces within three years. Three routes to this objective were suggested: (a) straight reductions down to zero; (b) staged reductions; down to 140 launchers in Europe in the first year, with proportionate reductions in Asia; halving the number again in the second year; zero in the third; and (c) begin with the elimination of all European arms, but limit SS-20s to Central Asia (where they could threaten China but not Japan) and then bring them down to zero after three years. Options (b) and (c) implied a possible area of compromise in not moving beyond the first-stage reductions.

By the summer Soviet sources were indicating a willingness to postpone the question of British and French forces and compromise on Asian SS-20s.

Appendices

4 The data question in INF

In INF there has been little argument on the detail of the figures themselves. At issue are the actual forces to be included. The United States has argued that only land-based missiles should be taken into account. The inclusion of aircraft would not suddenly change the overall picture, but it would complicate the negotiations because of problems of definition and verification. Submarine-launched missiles (including 400 *Poseidon* warheads assigned to NATO Supreme Allied Command) were excluded because their proper place was in START (on this the Russians agreed). Since the SS-20s are semi-mobile and so in principle could be moved from the Asian to the European part of the USSR in a crisis (although this would be something of a performance), the USA has argued that all of them should be taken into account. Lastly, the Americans have counted warheads rather than launchers, to take account of the three warheads on each SS-20. According to this count, the position in 1981 was that the Soviet Union had 599 launchers (351 SS-20s and 248 SS-4/5s) and 1,301 warheads (because of three on each SS-20), whereas the United States had none.

Since over a number of years the Soviet SS-4s and SS-5s were to be phased out, and NATO planned to deploy 464 cruise and 108 *Pershing* IIs, the position by early 1986 was:

	United States			Soviet Union	
Launchers		Warheads	Launchers		Warheads
Pershing	108	108	SS-20	441	1,323
Cruise	32	128	SS-5	120	120
Total	140	236	Total	561	1,443

Twenty-seven SS-20s which have been removed from bases facing Europe are still included, because there is no evidence that they have been destroyed. This brings the totals to 243 (+27) facing Western Europe and 171 facing the Far East.

The Soviet position has been somewhat different. At the start of the negotiations it worked on the basis of the following presentation of the balance: see table opposite.

It considered only systems that were part of the 'European balance'. It also counted launchers rather than warheads, and included aircraft and old SLBMs. This made a total of 975 Soviet systems. In order to

Appendices

Soviet presentation of the European nuclear balance (December 1981)

NATO			Warsaw Pact	
IRBMs				
	SSBS S-2 (France)	18	SS-20	243
			SS-4/5	253
SLBMs				
	MSBS M-20 (France)	80	SS-N-5	18
	Polaris A-3 (UK)	64		
Aircraft				
	FB-111 (US-based)	65	*Badger/*	
	F-111	172	*Blinder/*	
	F-4	246	*Backfire*	461
	A-6/A-7 (carrier-based)	240		
	Mirage IV A (France)	33		
	Vulcan B-2 (UK)	56		
	Total	974	Total	975

demonstrate an existing equality (prior to the arrival of cruise and *Pershing* missiles), these systems had to be shown to be facing a comparable number on the NATO side.

The first step was to argue for the inclusion of 162 British and French missiles. The difficulty here was that submarine-launched missiles should logically be discussed, if anywhere, at START, along with the comparable US SSBNs. The next step was to include aircraft. There was no problem with the 172 F-111s based in Britain, but the other aircraft in the Soviet list were awkward, because they appeared to contradict the USSR's own counting rules. These rules were the inclusion of all systems with a range above 1,000 kilometres within a defined geographical zone which was extraordinarily complicated. It took in more than just the European landmass, and encompassed the Asian part of Turkey and enough of the Asian part of the Soviet Union to put West Germany out of range of current SS-20 missile bases (but not enough to protect Norway, Greece and Turkey). In addition, it stretched into adjacent seas and oceans, taking in the whole of the Mediterranean and half of the Atlantic.

The 65 FB-111s, a heavier version of the F-111, are all based in the United States and are therefore well outside even the Soviet inclusion zone. So if these aircraft were to be included, then why not Soviet aircraft and missiles in the Soviet Far East? Likewise with carrier-based aircraft. At any time, around 60 A-6 and A-7 nuclear-capable aircraft were to be found on two carriers with the US Sixth Fleet in the Mediterranean, but

Appendices

the Soviet figures included the *total* US inventory, which they put at 240 (the real figure was closer to 200).

A difficulty of a different sort arose with the inclusion of F-4 aircraft. The maximum range in the case of the F-4 is 4,400 kilometres. This assumes flight at optimum altitude and speed, minimum load and no return to base. In combat, aircraft fly faster, often at lower altitudes than the optimum, carrying heavy loads, and hope to return to base. So a better measure is combat radius. Assuming high altitude in transit but then low altitude to penetrate air defences results in a figure of 750 kilometres for the F-4. Showing little confidence in their own air defences, the Russians argued that the F-111 would fly at a high altitude. This logic would also take in 550 SU-19 *Fencer* aircraft, generally assumed to have a combat radius well in excess of 1,000 kilometres. The Soviet response was that they intended to fly these aircraft continuously at low altitudes — an approach which would only make sense if they had to avoid their own air defences. If the range limit were lowered to take in the F-4s, then in total some 1,100 extra Soviet aircraft would also be sucked in. As a fallback the Russians said that most of the *Fencers*, or their other aircraft, were not intended for nuclear roles; but the same was true for US aircraft.

With the revival of the negotiations in 1985, Soviet spokesmen began to bring their figures up to date. In order to respond to NATO's discussion of

Soviet presentation of the European nuclear balance (1985)

	NATO	Warsaw Pact
Missile launchers		
	US: 209	243 (SS-20)
	Britain: 64	130 (SS-5)
	France: 114	
	387	373
Aircraft		
	US: 596	477
	France: 32	
	628	477
Launchers + aircraft		
	1,015	850
Nuclear charges		
	on missiles 739	860
	on aircraft 2,261	1,140
	Total 3,000	2,000

Appendices

warheads, Soviet figures for nuclear charges (a term usefully covering both missile warheads and aircraft-delivered bombs) were provided. The missile figures were raised on the NATO side to take account of the introduction of cruise and *Pershing* and new French SSBNs, and lowered on the Soviet side because of a further decline in SS-4s. The US aircraft tally was reduced, possibly to release some to help construct a separate Pacific balance. There was also recognition that the UK *Vulcan* bombers had been withdrawn.

Finally, it is not altogether clear how the 'charges' count has been constructed. It would appear for example that it is assumed that the new UK Chevaline front-end for its *Polaris* force has six warheads. Although the British government has never officially given a figure (except to say that it is no more than three), it is thought that the actual number is two.

5 Negotiating history of MBFR

1973

Preparatory talks began in the spring of 1973. The guidelines area was identified as consisting of the Benelux countries, West and East Germany, Poland and Czechoslovakia. France refused to have anything to do with the exercise, and Western attempts to include Hungary were rebuffed. Two categories of participants were established:

> *Direct participants.* Countries which have forces in Central Europe and are possible participants in reductions: from NATO, Belgium, Canada, West Germany, Luxembourg, the Netherlands, the United Kingdom and the United States; from the Warsaw Pact, Czechoslovakia, East Germany, Poland and the Soviet Union.
>
> *Non-direct participants.* Countries which do not have forces in Central Europe and would not participate in reductions under an agreement: from NATO, Denmark, Greece, Italy, Norway and Turkey; from the Warsaw Pact, Bulgaria, Hungary and Romania.

Actual negotiations began on 30 October 1973. The first proposal, which was tabled by the East on 8 November, presumed a satisfactory existing balance of strength, which it sought to preserve through equal reductions of roughly 17 per cent on each side, to be made in three phases. In phase one, 20,000 troops would be withdrawn on each side; 10,000 each by the USA and the USSR; 5,000 each by West and East Germany; and a further 5,000 for each alliance by the other participants. Phases two and three would see reductions of 5 per cent by NATO and 10 per cent by the

89

Appendices

Warsaw Pact. It was stipulated that both sides make reductions in entire units, including conventional and nuclear weapons (such as battlefield nuclear weapons, tanks, aircraft and other major systems); that forces from nations outside the reduction zone be withdrawn; that forces of nations within the zone be disbanded and removed; and that countries within the zone then be required to maintain national force and equipment levels at or below the post-reduction levels. The last requirement was essentially a device for enforcing a permanent ceiling on the West German armed forces.

The West tabled its first formal proposal on 22 November 1973. The objective was an overall parity in force levels to be achieved through reductions in two separate phases, with talks on phase two beginning only after phase one had been formalized. Only the superpowers would be involved in phase one, during which they would reduce their ground forces by 15 per cent. NATO figures declared this to mean 29,000 American and 68,000 Soviet troops. The Soviet reductions were to be in the form of a tank army of 68,000 men and 1,700 tanks. Phase two would involve all direct participants. Ground forces would be reduced to an eventual common ceiling on each side of about 700,000. NATO figures suggested that this would mean a reduction of 225,000 Warsaw Pact troops and 77,000 NATO troops in addition to the US/Soviet reductions in phase one. Finally, the West demanded a series of 'associated measures', including safeguard and verification procedures, the prevention of forces that had been withdrawn from reappearing in full strength in flank countries, and prior notification of movements of troops in the reduction area.

1975

A stalemate soon developed. On 16 December 1975, in an effort to break the deadlock, NATO tabled a new offer, known as Option III. The offer was to withdraw 1,000 US nuclear warheads, 54 nuclear-capable F-4 aircraft and 36 *Pershing* I missile launchers from Western Europe. In addition, NATO agreed to include air force manpower in the reductions by proposing a common ceiling of 900,000 air and ground forces (the East wanted separate ceilings). In return, the East was still required to withdraw a specified tank army with 1,700 tanks and to agree to full reductions on the basis of Western data. NATO also stipulated that Option III was a 'one-time offer', which could be withdrawn if the East did not respond fully.

1976

On 19 February 1976, the East responded, but not fully. It agreed to a

Appendices

two-phase reduction, with a first phase limited to US and Soviet troops, but not to the notion of two negotiating phases — both phases would have to be negotiated together. The Warsaw Pact was concerned that the first phase would impose limits on its largest army (i.e. the Soviet army), while the largest NATO army in Europe (i.e. the West German army), would remain unconstrained. For the same reason, the East refused to accept common ceilings and continued to demand national sub-ceilings for each of the direct participants.

During this period, the Warsaw Pact began to insist that parity (rather than a satisfactory if asymmetrical relationship) already existed. On 10 June 1976, to back up this claim, it tabled its first hard data. Its figures sharply diverged from those of NATO and led to a controversy which has yet to be settled (see Appendix 6).

1978

NATO tabled a new proposal on 19 April 1978, with two important concessions to the East: first, the USSR could make its reductions of 68,000 men and 1,700 tanks in the form of three divisions, rather than one complete tank army, though the numerical requirement remained; and, second, after agreement on a first phase, the West would make a firm pledge on second-phase reductions, which would still have to be negotiated separately.

On 8 June 1978, a new Eastern proposal accepted the West's ultimate goal of a common ceiling in the reduction area of approximately 900,000 ground and air forces, with a sub-ceiling of 700,000 for ground forces. However, the data discrepancies offset any real concession; the phase-one reductions would be of 30,000 Soviet and 14,000 US troops. The East offered only 1,000 tanks (and 250 armoured personnel carriers) for 1,000 NATO battlefield nuclear weapons (instead of the 1,700 requested by the West). It modified its position on national sub-ceilings with a complicated formula: after an agreement, NATO or Warsaw Pact members could increase ground forces by the equivalent of *half* any unilateral reductions made subsequently by another ally, provided that such increases did not bring the country's ground forces above the pre-agreement level. Lastly, as a gesture towards the concept of confidence-building measures, a ban on military exercises of more than 50–60,000 troops within the guidelines area was proposed. (This would happen to catch NATO exercises far more often than those of the Warsaw Pact.)

A further Warsaw Pact proposal of 30 November 1978 for a military freeze on the manpower levels of both sides in Central Europe, until a force reductions agreement could be negotiated, was rejected by NATO as confirming Eastern superiority in Europe.

Appendices

1979

In early 1979, in a secret approach to the United States, the Soviet Union suggested a bilateral agreement between Moscow and Washington dealing with phase-one reductions and preparing the ground for later reductions by their respective allies, who would be confronted with a *fait accompli*. To make this possible, it dropped its requirement that the other participants accept obligations on eventual reductions at the start of phase one, and now allowed a period of two to three years for phase-one withdrawals, in which the next stage could be negotiated. The data problems could be dealt with during this period, since they were not relevant to the phase-one withdrawals. It would consider US proposals on associated measures, but still insisted on national sub-ceilings and the trade between US nuclear weapons and Soviet tanks.

On 6 October 1979, as part of his 'peace offensive', President Brezhnev announced plans to withdraw unilaterally 20,000 troops and 1,000 tanks from East Germany. On 5 December 1979, the first unilateral Soviet troop and tank withdrawals were made ostentatiously from East Germany in the form of a unit of the Soviet 6th Armoured Division based in Wittenberg.

In December, NATO agreed to withdraw 1,000 US nuclear weapons (but not their associated delivery vehicles). Arguing that the USSR had never responded fully to its 'one-time offer', and that delivery vehicles could be dealt with in another forum, NATO now dropped Option III. A new and detailed NATO proposal was presented in Vienna on 20 December 1979.

Ground troop reductions in phase one would now be of the size proposed by the East: 13,000 US troops from West Germany and three Soviet army divisions totalling 30,000 men from Eastern Europe. (These figures were down from 29,000 and 68,000 respectively.) This concession was tied to agreements on the relevant data. The US/Soviet withdrawal would be linked with a non-binding commitment for later reductions by the other participating states. Other areas of controversy in armament reductions and limitations would be deferred until phase two, which would be abandoned if there were no agreement on overall data and reductions during phase one.

In addition, a package of specific associated measures would be established. These involved: (i) confirmation of the confidence-building measures of the CSCE Final Act by all MBFR participants; (ii) prior notification of any out-of-garrison activities at the divisional level within the guidelines area, on the flanks where there were common frontiers with the guidelines area (i.e. Turkey and Norway), and in a significant proportion of Soviet territory involving units of division size or larger; (iii) a compulsory exchange of observers to monitor such activities; (iv) prior notification within one calendar month of troop movements of division

Appendices

size or larger into the guidelines area from outside the area; (v) the establishment of permanent observers at designated entry and exit points to and from the guidelines area (e.g. ports, airfields, and major rail and road crossings) to monitor the flow of forces entering or leaving the guidelines area, with the additional requirement that all such movements be conducted through declared entry/exit points; (vi) the right on request, within a specified number of hours, to inspect any suspect activity within the guidelines area by means of mobile ground teams or low-altitude aerial observation flights (both helicopter and fixed-wing), with the number of such inspections per year to be limited; (vii) exchange of information on military data; (viii) non-interference with national means of surveillance; and (ix) a consultative mechanism with which to implement an MBFR agreement by using MBFR negotiating structures already in existence in Vienna.

1980

On 31 January 1980, negotiations resumed despite the Soviet invasion of Afghanistan. NATO warned that the talks had been placed in jeopardy, and little headway was made.

On 10 July 1980, a new Warsaw Pact proposal suggested that the East should be credited with the unilateral withdrawal of 20,000 Soviet troops in the multilateral agreement. The offer was now to withdraw 20,000 troops in Central Europe in return for 13,000 US troops — 10,000 less than the Pact's 1978 offer and the NATO proposal of December 1979. The Eastern claim was that in effect Soviet reductions would now be 40,000. A binding freeze on the forces of other participating countries during the implementation of phase one and the negotiation of phase two was still required, as was a new variation on the national sub-ceiling question. Now the size of the armed forces (ground and air) of any party to the agreement was not to exceed, in Central Europe, 50 per cent of the total collective levels of 900,000 men — that is, was not to be more than 450,000.

A further modification in 1983, to take account of the West's comments on associated measures, would allow observers to watch the evacuation of some forces (but apparently not the most substantial contingents), and three or four temporary monitoring posts to be established through which the troops involved in the reductions would pass. There would be mutual notification of the beginning and end of the reduction steps. Thereafter three or four permanent monitoring stations would be established through which all troops entering or leaving the guidelines area had to pass. There would be no right to on-site inspection, but it could be requested if some transgression were suspected and if the host country permitted. In addition, there were proposals for announcing exercises and troop

Appendices

movements of more than 20,000 troops. Manoeuvres would be limited to 40,000 to 50,000 troops. An appropriate consultative mechanism would be created and there would be periodic exchanges of statistical data. More general measures, such as the extension of the guidelines area and notification and observation of out-of-garrison activities, were rejected. The CSCE was suggested as the proper forum for the discussion of other ideas.

1985

In February 1985, the Warsaw Pact submitted a new package with the same figures of 20,000 Soviet and 13,000 US troops. However, this withdrawal would now be part of a binding, verified agreement rather than simply by mutual example. The package also recognized a NATO requirement that 90 per cent of the troops be withdrawn as units rather than as individuals. There was a shift from the early insistence on the two phases being kept close together. The initial cuts would avoid the tricky data question, but thereafter this question could not be avoided.

NATO's response, tabled in December 1985, proposed a first-step reduction of 5,000 US and 11,500 Soviet troops. The two sides would reduce their numbers as soon as possible, after which all forces would be held at the reduced levels for three years. During this time there would be a rigid monitoring regime: exchange of data, observers at entry and exit points, and 30 inspections a year (25 for ground troops, 5 for airbases). This would facilitate verification of statements on data.

The initial reductions had become virtually irrelevant, and were purely symbolic. The real issue now was verification. NATO was offering the Warsaw Pact the chance to 'adjust' its numbers as part of the initial reductions. Only the reduced numbers would be verified. If the Warsaw Pact figures for its own forces were correct, this would be revealed by the NATO inspections; if they were not, the Warsaw Pact had the option, when formally reducing its 11,500 troops, also to withdraw an amount covering the difference between its claimed numbers and the NATO estimate (some 200,000 men).

On 14 February, the Soviet Union tabled a new draft treaty, in which it brought its figures for US/Soviet reductions down to 11,000 for the USSR and 6,500 for the USA (still not quite in line with NATO proposals). Armaments were still included. It made little movement on verification, and described NATO's requirements as 'over-bloated'. More significant was a speech made two months later by Mr Gorbachev in which he made it clear that he expected little from the Vienna talks. His proposal for a new forum contained many long-standing Soviet objectives. Its most interesting feature was a guidelines area from the 'Atlantic to the Urals'. If this meant only NATO and Warsaw Pact forces, there would be some advantages for NATO, given the much more attractive guidelines area and the opportunity to escape from the constraints of the data question. However, the basic problem of asymmetry would remain. It was suggested that these talks could either involve a new forum, or, more appropriately, come within the second stage of the Stockholm Conference on Disarmament in Europe. Warsaw Pact proposals envisaged cuts of 100,000 to 150,000 ground and air troops within two years followed by 25 per cent reductions in alliance strengths, backed by data exchange, control posts and some on-site inspection. NATO set up a task force to seek 'bold new steps . . . in the field of arms control'. All this suggested that MBFR itself was drawing to an empty conclusion.

6 The data question in MBFR

When the talks opened in 1973, NATO tabled the following data for ground forces in the guidelines area, including France: Warsaw Pact, 925,000; NATO, 770,000; disparity, 155,000. These figures were not challenged by the Warsaw Pact, which seemed in the discussions, albeit implicitly, to accept the disparity.

In 1976, both sides tabled data on their own forces to a 1 January 1976 baseline. NATO's figures (which this time excluded France) showed 731,000, an increase of 14,000 for the relevant countries. The Pact data suggested that it had only 805,000 ground troops. NATO said that its estimates of Warsaw Pact troops exceeded this by more than 150,000 (its own estimates — untabled — were in the region of 962,000).

Warsaw Pact figures showed virtual equality instead of Pact superiority. NATO complained that the original presentation was insufficiently detailed. More figures were provided in spring 1978, still to a 1 January 1976 baseline, and they were followed by new estimates tabled by NATO.

In June 1980, both sides tabled new data, again only on their own forces, to a 1 January 1980 baseline. The new Warsaw Pact figures were:

Country	Ground	Air	Total
USSR	423,300*	40,500	463,800*
East Germany	93,000	29,800	122,800
Poland	161,800*	67,300	229,100*
Czechoslovakia	137,100	44,700	181,800
	815,200*	182,300	997,500*

*changed from last estimate

Warsaw Pact data and NATO estimates on Pact forces in the guidelines area as of 1 January 1976

PACT DATA[a]

Country	Ground	Air	Total	
USSR	426,300	40,500	466,800	
East Germany	93,000	29,800	122,800	
Poland	148,600	67,300	215,900	
Czechoslovakia	137,100	44,700	181,800	
	805,000	182,300	987,300	

NATO ESTIMATES[b]

Country	Ground	Air	Total	Discrepancy in totals
USSR	483,300[c]	46,300	529,600	62,800
East Germany	111,000	52,800	163,800	41,000
Poland	220,100[d]	84,200	304,300	88,400
Czechoslovakia	141,800	35,800	177,600	(4,200)[e]
	956,200	219,100	1,175,300	188,000

[a] Tabled in Vienna from 15 March to 4 April 1978.
[b] Ground force data tabled in Vienna from 7 November to 12 December 1978; data on air forces tabled from 20 February to 10 April 1979.
[c] Assumes 90% manning levels of Soviet motorized rifle and tank divisions.
[d] Assumes 70% manning levels of Polish motorized rifle and tank divisions.
[e] Pact data on Czech force levels exceeded NATO estimates.

Source: Jeffrey Record, *Force Reductions in Europe: Starting Over* (Cambridge, Mass., Institute for Foreign Policy Analysis, 1980), p. 56.

Appendices

In tabling this data, the Warsaw Pact explained that the Polish increase was not a real increase but resulted from taking account of Western arguments and adding elements not previously included. The new figures increased admitted Pact levels by 10,200 and therefore made little dent on the disparity. There was little disagreement on the size of NATO forces.

In October 1980, the Warsaw Pact unilaterally tabled new data for the Soviet Union, to a 1 August 1980 baseline, giving 404,800. The reduction of 18,500 was claimed to be the balance of the unilateral withdrawal of troops from East Germany announced in October 1979, the other 1,500 having been withdrawn before 1 January 1980.

NATO has not tabled updated estimates of Eastern forces to any 1980 baseline. However, NATO's current estimate for the total would appear to be 1,210,000 troops (970,000 ground and 240,000 air). This represents an increase of some 14,000 ground and 21,000 air troops since 1980, and a discrepancy of some 200,000.

According to NATO figures, the discrepancy represents 16 per cent of the total and is higher than any actual proposed reductions. NATO officials are confident of their estimates and that the discrepancy is well outside the normal margin of error. The Pact explanations of the discrepancy have suggested that its own data exclude military and paramilitary personnel involved in functions performed by civilians on the NATO side, despite the fact that, when presenting its figures in 1976, it confirmed that all military personnel were included, regardless of missions or functions. The Pact has also argued that NATO figures exaggerate manning levels.

It should be noted that although Soviet forces account for about half of the Warsaw Pact total, the discrepancy here is equivalent to only about one-third of the total discrepancy (and about 12 per cent of the total Soviet figure). The most dramatic discrepancies occur with the Polish and East German forces, with gaps of 40 per cent and 33 per cent, respectively, between NATO and Warsaw Pact data. However, the extra Soviet forces are more of a mystery because, as outside forces, they do not have the extra 'hangers on' accumulated by forces at home bases.

Appendices

7 Negotiating history of the Conference on Confidence and Security Building Measures and Disarmament

1975

The Final Act of the 1975 Conference on Security and Cooperation in Europe agreed joint confidence-building measures. These measures were limited. The 35 signatory states undertook to provide notification, not less than 21 days in advance, of their ground-force manoeuvres (with or without air and naval components) which exceeded a total of 25,000 personnel. There were also provisions for discretionary notification of sub-threshold manoeuvres and military movements, and for the discretionary invitation of observers to manoeuvres of any size.

A variety of proposals for extending CBMs were developed for the 1977–8 Belgrade review conference, but they got lost in the general tangle over human rights. Proposals for the Madrid review conference, which began in 1980, were more elaborate and were promoted more vigorously.

1978

President Giscard d'Estaing, at the 1978 United Nations Special Session on Disarmament, proposed a separate Conference on Disarmament in Europe, to be developed through two stages: first, a broadening of existing CBMs (which would be made mandatory) to cover extra military movements and transfers of information, plus an extension of the area of their application to the Urals; and, second, the discussion within this guidelines area of actual limitations on conventional forces, such as tanks, artillery and aircraft.

A modified version of this approach was adopted by NATO. The first stage followed established policy, but there were worries about the second stage: it undercut the NATO position in the MBFR talks; the deliberate exclusion of nuclear weapons was artificial; and, finally, 35 diverse nations addressing the whole range of modern armaments would be a diplomatic monstrosity. The Americans were unhappy about separating disarmament from the rest of the CSCE package (from human rights to various forms of cooperation), since they believed it might let the Russians off the human-

Appendices

rights hook while providing them with a new propaganda forum. They wanted progress on a new conference to depend at each stage on decisions at a full CSCE review conference. One of the first pro-arms-control acts of the new Reagan administration in February 1981 was to endorse the French proposal, which now de-emphasized the second phase.

At Madrid, NATO proposals for this new conference concentrated on making the voluntary measures obligatory (including all out-of-garrison activities by units above divisional level) and, crucially, extending the area in which CBMs were expected to operate from the CSCE limits of only 250 kilometres into Soviet territory to the geographical limits of Europe at the Urals. This last measure would multiply by ten the area of the Soviet Union covered by CBMs.

1979

The Warsaw Pact proposal, first put forward in May 1979, was for a conference on military detente and disarmament in Europe, separate from the CSCE exercise and offering a vague agenda.

1981

In his 23 February 1981 speech to the XXVI Party Congress, President Brezhnev conceded that European Russia could be covered by CBMs on condition that the Western states similarly enlarged their own zone of application. The meaning of this last phrase was not altogether clear.

The Soviet Union's own proposals were directed against improvements in NATO's overall position; for example, forbidding additions to alliances (e.g., Spanish membership of NATO), or additional military bases (with new cruise missile deployments in mind). Its main proposal concerning the CBMs already instituted was to limit all manoeuvres to 40,000–50,000 troops. In his 23 February speech, Brezhnev also said that the USSR was prepared to give notice of air and sea exercises.

1983

The Madrid conference came to a close in September 1983 at a final meeting overshadowed by the row over the shooting down by Soviet air defences of a Korean airliner (an unfortunate prelude to a discussion on confidence-building!). It was agreed to establish a new 35-nation conference to meet in Stockholm from January 1984 under the title 'Conference on Confidence and Security Building Measures and Disarmament in Europe'. NATO countries tend to refer to it as the CDE

Appendices

(Conference on Disarmament in Europe), thereby reflecting the original French inspiration though no longer their major concern.

The mandate for the conference by and large met NATO requirements: it would cover all Europe up to the Urals; the first stage would be concerned with what were now called confidence and security building measures; and there would then be a report back to the next CSCE review conference in Vienna at the end of 1986. That conference would determine whether or not to move on to a new stage.

1984

The conference opened on 17 January 1984 in Stockholm. A week later, Turkey formally introduced the NATO position, which was based on six proposals: (1) exchange of information at the start of each year on air and ground forces in the zone of application; (2) exchange of annual forecasts of all military activities in the CDE area which would be notifiable in advance under other measures; (3) forty-five days' notice for (a) out-of-garrison activities involving 6,000 or more ground troops, (b) mobilization activities involving 25,000 or more troops, and (c) amphibious activities involving 3,000 or more troops in a landing in the zone; (4) the invitation of observers for all participating states to all pre-notified activities; (5) no interference with national technical means of verification; and (6) improved arrangements for communication between participating states. The Warsaw Pact delegates described these proposals as legitimizing spying.

The Soviet approach was outlined at the end of January 1984. It also involved six points, but they were of a far more general and fundamental nature than those of NATO: (1) no first use of nuclear weapons; (2) a non-aggression pact; (3) limitation on military expenditures; (4) a European chemical zone; (5) nuclear-weapon-free zones; and (6) a willingness to elaborate on 'limitation and notification of military manoeuvres'. Later they identified some CBMs involving limitation on the scale of exercises and notification of exercises above a certain threshold, and emphasized that these should include major air and sea exercises.

In March, eight NNA countries submitted a joint proposal. This accepted most of NATO's themes on prior notification and exchange of observers, but also picked up the Soviet interest in limitation on military expenditures and the non-use of force.

In the sessions the West argued that political confidence would flow from both sides making their force structures more transparent, since greater transparency would rule out a surprise attack. The East insisted that without a prior improvement in political confidence, measures

Appendices

designed to increase transparency could be viewed as an aid to *preparation* for surprise attack.

In June, President Reagan agreed to talk about the non-use of force. He stated that, 'if discussions on reaffirming the principle in which we believe so deeply will bring the Soviet Union to negotiate agreements which will give concrete new meaning to that principle, we will gladly enter into such discussions'. NATO hoped that a willingness to discuss the non-use of force would make possible a serious negotiation on its own proposals, despite the fact that such declarations would have little meaning in practice and have anyway already been made via the UN Charter. The initial Eastern response was to claim that this did not go far enough, for it did not include nuclear weapons.

The next month the NNA group proposed two separate working-groups. One would work at the military/technical issues, and divide further into two sub-groups on notification and observation; the other group would look at political measures. NATO accepted this; the Warsaw Pact reserved its position. Eventually in December it was agreed to set up two working-groups: Group A would deal with political CBMs, constraints on military forces, forecasts and the provision of information; and Group B would cover all measures tabled on observers and notification of exercises.

1985

In discussions during 1985, the various proposals were given greater precision. The Warsaw Pact provided more detail on its proposed CBMs. There would be prior notification, 30 days in advance of air force manoeuvres with more than 200 aircraft, naval exercises with more than 30 warships and 100 aircraft, and major land exercises with more than 20,000 troops.

These proposals touched on one of the more controversial aspects of the conference's mandate. NATO insisted that only air and sea exercises directly related to European security should be discussed, whereas the Soviet Union wished to discuss anything underway in the adjoining air and sea space.

The first indications of a compromise came with the buildup to the November 1985 summit. In his Paris speech of 3 October, Gorbachev agreed on mutual exchanges of annual plans for military activity that was subject to notification. In mid-October the areas for compromise were identified and five sub-groups set up to begin drafting. These areas were: renunciation of force; announcement and observation of military activities; restrictive measures; exchange of annual forecasts; and information, verification, communication and consultation. The East had not insisted on its proposals on nuclear-free and chemical zones, military budgets and

Appendices

no first use of nuclear weapons. The West had given up its proposed exchange of information.

At the November summit, Reagan and Gorbachev stated their intention to facilitate an early and successful completion of the work of the conference. To this end, they reaffirmed the need for a document which would include mutually acceptable confidence and security building measures and give concrete expression to, and put into effect, the principle of the non-use of force.

1986

It took until the middle of the year for the momentum of the negotiations to revive. The USSR agreed that only air and sea exercises linked with ground manoeuvres be included. There were hints of compromise on the threshold for notification of manoeuvres (12,000 troops). The main stumbling-block was the inspection regime, with the USSR insisting on a right to refuse on-site inspection.